The Psychology of Investing

The Psychology of Investing

SECOND EDITION

John R. Nofsinger
Washington State University

PEARSON
Prentice Hall

Upper Saddle River, New Jersey 07458

Library of Congress Cataloging-in-Publication Data

Nofsinger, John R.
The psychology of investing / John R. Nofsinger.—2nd ed.
p. cm.
Includes bibliographical references and index.
ISBN 0-13-143270-2 (pbk.)
I. Investments—Psychological aspects. I. Title.

HG4515.15.N643 2005
332.6'01'9—dc22

2004044409

Senior Acquisitions Editor: Jackie Aaron
Editor-in-Chief: Jeff Shelstad
Editorial Assistant: Francesca Calogero
Executive Marketing Manager: Debbie Clare
Marketing Assistant: Amanda Fisher
Managing Editor: John Roberts
Production Editor: Maureen Wilson
Manufacturing Buyer: Michelle Klein
Cover Design: Jayne Conte
Cover Illustration/Photo: Rob Colvin/Stock Illustration Source, Inc.
Composition: Laserwords
Full-Service Project Management: Jennifer Welsch, BookMasters, Inc.

Credits and acknowledgments borrowed from other sources and reproduced, with permission, in this textbook appear on appropriate page within text.

Pearson Education LTD.
Pearson Education Australia PTY, Limited
Pearson Education Singapore, Pte. Ltd
Pearson Education North Asia Ltd
Pearson Education, Canada, Ltd
Pearson Educación de Mexico, S.A. de C.V.
Pearson Education–Japan
Pearson Education Malaysia, Pte. Ltd

PEARSON
Prentice
Hall

10 9 8 7
ISBN 0–13–143270–2

Contents

Preface

An old Wall Street adage states that two factors move the market: fear and greed. Although true, this characterization is far too simplistic. The human mind is so sophisticated and human emotions are so complex that the emotions of fear and greed do not adequately describe the psychology that affects people as they make investment decisions. This book is one of the first texts to delve into this fascinating and important subject.

Few other texts provide this information because traditional finance has focused on developing the tools that investors use to optimize expected return and risk. This endeavor has been fruitful, yielding tools such as asset pricing models, portfolio theories, and option pricing. Although investors should use these tools in their investment decision making, they typically do not. This is because psychology affects our decisions more than financial theory does.

Unfortunately, psychological biases inhibit one's ability to make good investment decisions. By learning about your psychological biases, you can overcome them and increase your wealth. You will notice that most of the chapters in this book are structured similarly. A psychological bias is first described and illustrated with everyday behavior (like driving a car). The effect of the bias on investment decisions is then explained. Last, academic studies are used to show that investors do indeed exhibit the problem.

What we know about investor psychology is increasing rapidly. This second edition of *The Psychology of Investing* is expanded by 20 percent, with new evidence and ideas added to every chapter. Also, Chapter 8 has been rewritten to focus more on the role of human interaction in the investment process. Finally, an entirely new chapter has been included on the influence of feelings and mood on financial decision making.

This material does not replace the investment texts of traditional finance. Understanding psychological biases complements the traditional finance tools. Indeed, after reading this book, you should be convinced that traditional tools are valuable.

The Psychology of Investing

CHAPTER 1

Psychology and Finance

Traditionally, a formal education in finance has dismissed the idea that one's personal psychology can be a detriment in making good investment decisions. For the past three decades, the field of finance has evolved based on the following two assumptions.

- People make rational decisions.
- People are unbiased in their predictions about the future.

By assuming that people act in their own best interests, the finance field has been able to create some powerful tools for investors. For example, investors can use modern portfolio theory to obtain the highest expected return possible for any given level of risk they can bear. Pricing models (such as the Capital Asset Pricing Model [CAPM], the Arbitrage Pricing Theory [APT], and option pricing) can help value securities and provide insights into expected risks and returns. Investment texts are full of these useful theories.

However, psychologists have known for a long time that these are bad assumptions. People often act in a seemingly irrational manner and make predictable errors in their forecasts.

The finance field has been slow to accept the possibility that economic decisions could be predictably biased. Early proponents of behavioral finance often were considered heretics. Over the last decade though, the evidence that psychology and emotions influence financial decisions became more convincing. Today, the early proponents of behavioral finance are no longer heretics, but visionaries. Although the controversies of when, how, and why psychology affects investing continue, many believe that the 2002 Nobel Prize in Economics awards to psychologist Daniel Kahneman and experimental economist Vernon Smith have vindicated the field.

Financial economists are now realizing that investors can be irrational. Indeed, predictable decision errors by investors can affect the function of the markets. Most importantly, people's reasoning errors affect their investing, and ultimately their wealth. Investors who understand the tools of modern investing still can fail as investors if they let psychological biases control their decisions. By reading this book, you should:

- Learn many psychological biases that affect decision making.
- Understand how these biases affect investment decisions.
- See how these decisions reduce your wealth.
- Learn to recognize and avoid them in your own life.

The rest of this chapter will illustrate that these psychological problems are real. The arguments will be far more convincing if you participate in the following two demonstrations.

A SIMPLE ILLUSTRATION

One example of the reasoning mistakes caused by the brain is the visual illusion. Consider the optical illusion in Figure 1.1.[1] Of the two horizontal lines, which looks longer?

In fact, both lines are the same length. Look again. Although you now know that the horizontal lines are equal in length, the top line still *looks* longer. Just knowing about the illusion does not eliminate it. However, if you had to make some decision based on these lines, knowing that it is an illusion would help you avoid a mistake.

FIGURE 1.1 Optical Illusion

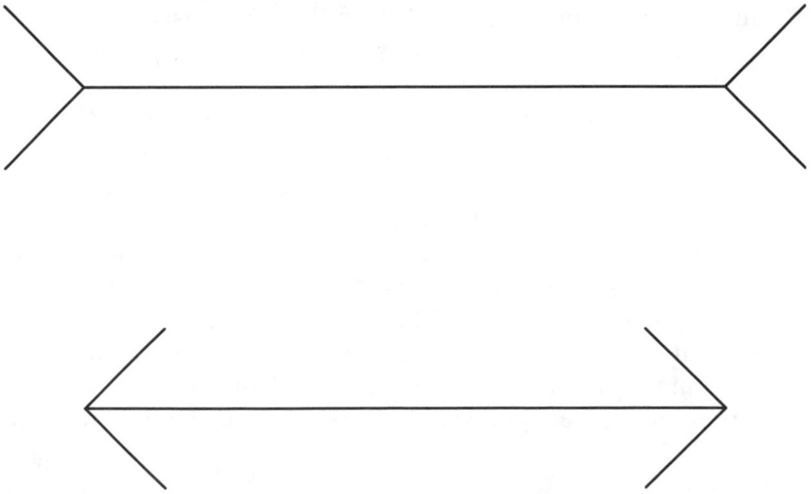

The brain does not work like a computer. Instead, it frequently processes information through shortcuts and emotional filters to shorten analysis time. The decision arrived upon through this process is often not the same decision you would make without these filters. These filters and shortcuts can be referred to as psychological biases. Knowing about these psychological biases is the first step toward avoiding them. One common problem is overestimating the precision and importance of information. The following demonstration illustrates this problem.

PREDICTION

Let's face it, investing is difficult. You must make decisions based on information that might be inadequate or inaccurate. Additionally, you must understand and analyze the information effectively. Unfortunately, people make predictable errors in their forecasts.

Consider the 10 questions in Table 1.1.[2] Although you probably do not know the answers to these questions, enter the most probable range based on your best estimate. Specifically, give your best low guess and your best high guess so that you are 90 percent sure the answer lies somewhere between the two. Don't make the range so

TABLE 1.1 Enter the Range (Minimum and Maximum) for Which You Are 90 Percent Certain the Answer Lies Within

	Min.	*Max.*
1. What is the average weight of the adult blue whale, in pounds?	____	____
2. In what year was the Mona Lisa painted by Leonardo da Vinci?	____	____
3. How many independent countries were there at the end of 2000?	____	____
4. What is the air distance, in miles, between Paris, France, and Sydney, Australia?	____	____
5. How many bones are in the human body?	____	____
6. How many total combatants were killed in World War I?	____	____
7. How many books were in the Library of Congress at the end of 2000?	____	____
8. How long, in miles, is the Amazon river?	____	____
9. How fast does the earth spin (miles per hour) at the equator?	____	____
10. How many transistors are in the Pentium III computer processor?	____	____
	____	____

wide that the answer is guaranteed to lay within the range, but also don't make the range too narrow. If you consistently choose a range following these instructions, you should expect to get 9 of the 10 questions correct. Go ahead, give it your best shot.

If you have no idea of the answer to a question, then your range should be large to be 90 percent confident. On the other hand, if you think you can give a good educated guess, then you can choose a smaller range to be 90 percent confident. Now let's check the answers. They are: (1) 250,000 pounds, (2) 1,513, (3) 191 countries, (4) 10,543 miles, (5) 206 bones, (6) 8.3 million, (7) 18 million, (8) 4,000 miles, (9) 1,044 miles per hour, and (10) 9.5 million. Count your response correct if the answer lies between your low and high guesses. How many did you get right?

Most people miss five or more questions. However, if you are 90 percent sure of your range, then you should have missed only one. The fact is that you are too certain about your answers, even when you have no information or knowledge about the topic. Even being educated in probability is no help. Most finance professors miss at least five of the questions, too.

This demonstration illustrates that people have difficulty evaluating the precision of their knowledge and information. Now that you see the difficulty, you can have a chance to redeem yourself. Because this book relates psychology to investing, consider the following question.

> In 1896, the Dow Jones Industrial Average (DJIA) was at 40. At the end of 1998, the DJIA was at 9,181. The DJIA is a price-weighted average. Dividends are omitted from the index. What would the DJIA average have been at the end of 1998 if the dividends were reinvested each year?

Notice that Table 1.1 has room for your DJIA minimum and maximum guesses. Again, you should be 90 percent sure that the correct value lies within the range you choose.

Because you are 90 percent sure that the correct value lies within the range you chose, you should get this one correct. Are you ready for the answer? If dividends were reinvested in the DJIA, the average would have been 652,230 at the end of 1998.[3] Does this surprise you? It surprises most people. Even after learning that most people set their range too narrowly in their prediction and experiencing the problem first hand, most people continue to do it.

This example also illustrates another aspect of investor psychology called anchoring. When you read the question, you focused on the DJIA price level of 9,181; that is, you anchored your thinking to

9,181. You probably made your guess by starting at this anchor and then trying to add an appropriate amount to compensate for the dividends. Investors anchor on their stock purchase price and the recent highest stock price.

LONG TERM CAPITAL MANAGEMENT

Even Nobel prize winners in the field of economics are prone to overestimating the precision of their knowledge. Consider the plight of the hedge fund Long Term Capital Management (LTCM). The partners of the fund included John Meriwether, the famed bond trader from Salomon Brothers; David Mullins, a former vice-chairman of the Federal Reserve Board; and Nobel prize winners Myron Scholes and Robert Merton. The firm employed 24 people with doctoral degrees.

The hedge fund began in 1994 and enjoyed stellar returns. In the beginning of 1998, LTCM had $4 billion in equity. It also had borrowed $100 billion to leverage its positions for higher returns. Its main strategy was to find arbitrage opportunities in the bond market.

In August of 1998, Russia devalued its currency and defaulted on some of its debt. This action started a chain of events over the next four weeks that led to devaluation in many emerging countries. Bond and stock markets throughout the world declined. The prices of U.S. Treasury securities skyrocketed as investors fled to the safest investments.

The equity in the LTCM portfolio fell from $4 billion to $0.6 billion in one month. The Federal Reserve Bank feared that a margin call on LTCM would force it to liquidate its $100 billion worth of positions. Selling these positions during this precarious time might have precipitated a crisis that could endanger the financial system. By late September, a consortium of leading investment banks and commercial banks injected $3.5 billion into the fund in exchange for 90 percent of the equity.[4]

How could a hedge fund with such brainpower lose 90 percent of its equity in one month? Apparently, in designing their models, the partners did not think so many things could go wrong at the same time. It appears that they set their range of possible outcomes too narrow.

BEHAVIORAL FINANCE

Even the smartest people are affected by psychological biases, but traditional finance has considered this irrelevant. Traditional finance assumes that people are "rational" and tells us how people should behave in order to maximize their wealth. These ideas have brought us arbitrage theory, portfolio theory, asset pricing theory, and option pricing theory.

Alternatively, behavioral finance studies how people actually behave in a financial setting.[5] Specifically, it is the study of how psychology affects financial decisions, corporations, and the financial markets. This book focuses on a subset of these issues—how psychological biases affect investors. The investor who truly understands these biases also will appreciate more fully the tools traditional finance has provided.

SOURCES OF COGNITIVE ERRORS

Many of the behaviors of investors are outcomes of *prospect theory*. This theory describes how people frame and value a decision involving uncertainty.[6] First, investors frame the choices in terms of potential gains and losses relative to a specific reference point. Although investors seem to anchor on various reference points, the purchase price appears to be important. Second, investors value the gains/losses according to an *S*-shaped function as shown in Figure 1.2.

Notice several things about the value function in the figure. First, the function is concave for gains. Investors feel good (i.e., have higher utility) when they make a $500 gain. They feel better when they make a $1,000 gain. However, they do not feel twice as good when they gain $1,000 as when they gain $500.

Second, notice that the function is convex for taking a loss. This means that investors feel bad when they have a loss, but twice the loss does not make them feel twice as bad.

Third, the function is steeper for losses than for gains. This asymmetry between gains and losses leads to different reactions in dealing with winning and losing positions. (See Chapter 3.)

An additional aspect of prospect theory is that people segregate each investment in order to track gains and losses and periodically reexamine positions. These separate accounts are referred to as *mental accounting*.[7] (See Chapter 5.) Viewing each investment separately rather than using a portfolio approach limits investors' ability to minimize risk and maximize return. (See Chapter 6.)

A different approach to the psychology of investing is to categorize behavioral biases by their source.[8] Some cognitive errors result from *self-deception*, which occurs because people tend to think they are better than they really are. This self-deception helps them fool others and thus survive the natural selection process. Another source

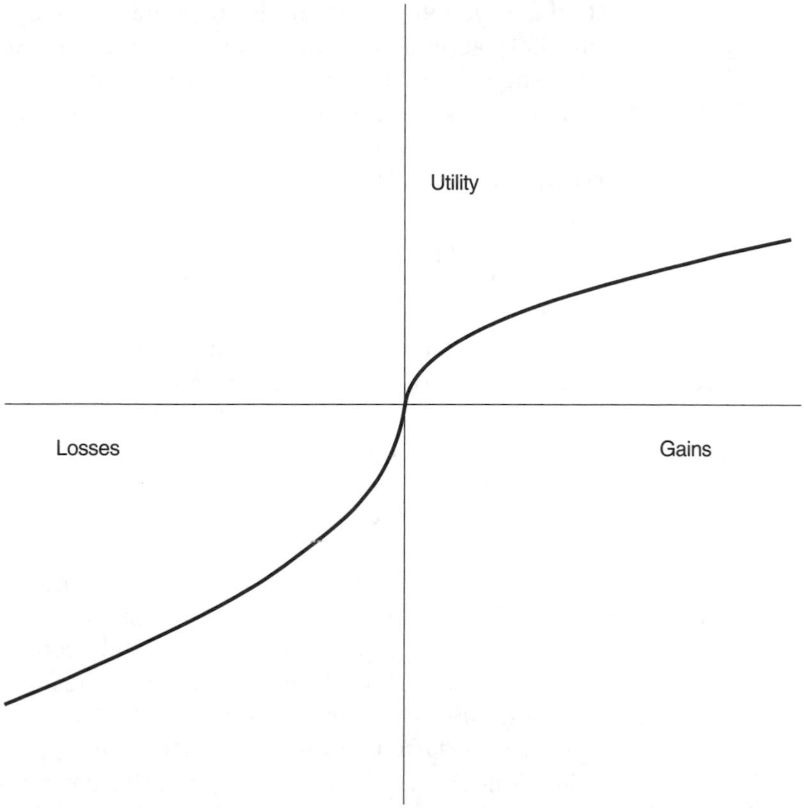

FIGURE 1.2 Prospect Theory Value Function

of bias comes from *heuristic simplification*. Simply stated, heuristic simplification exists because constraints on cognitive resources (like memory, attention, and processing power) force the brain to shortcut complex analyses. Prospect theory is considered an outcome of heuristic simplification. A third source of bias comes from a person's *mood,* which can overcome reason.

Human interaction and peer effects are also important in financial decision making. Human interactions are how people share information and communicate feelings about the information. The cues obtained about the opinions and emotions of others influence one's decisions.

WHAT TO EXPECT

The next six chapters of this book discuss psychological biases that affect people's daily lives. These chapters are all structured in a similar manner. First, the psychological trait is identified and explained using common, daily activities as examples. Second, the results of research studies show how the bias affects real people. Last, the degree to which investors are affected by the bias is examined.

Chapters 2, 3, and 4 demonstrate how investment decision making is affected by emotions. As demonstrated in the previous example, people set their range of possible outcomes too narrow. This is part of a self-deception problem called *overconfidence*. Overconfident investors trade too much, take too much risk, and earn lower returns. This topic is discussed in Chapter 2. Chapter 3 illustrates how investors' views of themselves cause them to avoid feelings of regret and instead seek pride. Consequently, investors sell winner stocks too soon and hold on to loser stocks too long. Last, Chapter 3 demonstrates that your past failures and successes have a dramatic impact on your current decision-making process. Indeed, your memory of the past might change over time to soften your regret over failures.

Chapters 5 through 7 demonstrate how heuristic simplification affects the investor. For example, every day you are bombarded by information. The brain uses a process called mental accounting to store and keep track of important decisions and outcomes. Chapter 5 shows that the consequences of this process are that people make poor financial decisions. Discussed in Chapter 6 is one particularly important implication—how investors view portfolio diversification. The brain also uses shortcuts to process information quickly. These shortcuts create a tainted view of the information. This leads to the investor problems of representativeness and familiarity, which are discussed in Chapter 7.

The last three chapters are a little different. Chapter 8 discusses how investing has entered our social culture. The interaction between psychology, group psychology, and investing can contribute to market mania and price bubbles. The Internet also interacts with these factors to magnify the psychological biases. This is important because investors are influenced by the decisions being made around them. Chapter 9 focuses on the role of emotions and mood in the decision-making process. An investor's general level of optimism or pessimism influences his or her trading decisions. Last, Chapter 10 discusses the difficulty of maintaining self-control in the face of these psychological biases. Planning, incentives, and rules of thumb are helpful in avoiding common problems. Strategies for overcoming these problems are proposed.

Questions

1. Why might the traditional assumption of rational decision making make sense for investors?
2. Name four aspects of prospect theory.
3. Describe three sources of cognitive errors other than prospect theory.

End Notes

1. This is an old psychology example. However, the illusion is discussed in Daniel Kahneman and Mark Riepe, "Aspects of Investor Psychology," *Journal of Portfolio Management* (Summer 1998): 52–65.
2. This exercise is similar to one proposed by Edward Russo and Paul Shoemaker in *Decision Traps* (New York: Simon & Schuster, 1989) and a presentation by Hersh Shefrin at the 2000 Financial Management Association in Seattle, WA.
3. This analysis is done in Roger Clarke and Meir Statman, "The DJIA Crossed 652,230," *Journal of Portfolio Management* (Winter 2000): 89–93.
4. See "All Bets Are Off: How the Salesmanship and Brainpower Failed at Long Term Capital," *Wall Street Journal,* Nov. 16, 1998: A1.
5. See the discussion in Meir Statman, "Behavioral Finance: Past Battles and Future Engagements," *Financial Analysts Journal* (Nov./Dec. 1999): 18–27. I use the term *traditional finance* where Meir uses the term *standard finance*.
6. See Daniel Kahneman and Amos Tversky, "Prospect Theory: An Analysis of Decision Under Risk, *Econometrica* 46(1979): 171–185.
7. See Richard Thaler, "Mental Accounting and Consumer Choice," *Marketing Science* 4(1985): 199–214.
8. See David Hirshleifer, "Investor Psychology and Asset Pricing," *Journal of Finance* 56(2001): 1533–1597.

CHAPTER 2

Overconfidence

People can be overconfident. Psychologists have determined that overconfidence causes people to overestimate their knowledge, underestimate risks, and exaggerate their ability to control events. Does overconfidence occur in investment decision making? Security selection is a difficult task. It is precisely this type of task in which people exhibit the greatest degree of overconfidence. Are you overconfident?

Question: Are you a good driver? Compared with the drivers you encounter on the road, are you above average, average, or below average?

How did you answer this question? If overconfidence were not involved, approximately one third of you would answer above average, one third would say average, and one third would say below average. However, people are overconfident in their abilities. In one published study, 82 percent of the sampled college students rated themselves above average in driving ability.[1] Clearly, many of them are mistaken.

Many of those students were mistaken because they were overconfident about their driving skills. Being overconfident about driving might not be a problem that affects your life, but people are overconfident about their skills in many things. This overconfidence can even affect your financial future.

Consider this financially oriented example. Starting a business is a risky venture; in fact, most new businesses fail. When 2,994 new business owners were asked about their chances of success, they thought they had a 70 percent chance of success, but only 39 percent thought that any business like theirs would be as likely to succeed.[2] Why do new business owners think they have nearly twice the chance of success as others? They are overconfident.

Interestingly, people are more overconfident when they feel like they have control of the outcome—even when this is clearly not the case. For example, it is documented that if people are asked to bet on whether a coin toss is heads or tails, most bet larger amounts if the coin has yet to be tossed. That is, if the coin is tossed and the outcome is concealed, people will offer lower amounts when asked for bets. On the other hand, if asked for the bet before the toss, people tend to bet higher amounts. People act as if their involvement will somehow affect the outcome of the toss.[3] In this case, control of the outcome is clearly an illusion. This perception occurs in investing, as well. Even without information, people believe the stocks they own will perform better than stocks they do not own. However, ownership of a stock only gives the illusion of having control of the performance of the stock.

A Gallup/Paine Webber survey of individual investors conducted in early 2001 demonstrates this overconfidence. Of particular note is that many of those surveyed had recently experienced some negative outcomes after the technology stock bubble collapsed. When asked what they thought the stock market return would be during the next 12 months, the average answer was 10.3 percent. When asked what return they expected to earn on their portfolios, the average response was 11.7 percent. Typically, investors expect to earn an above-average return.

HOW OVERCONFIDENCE AFFECTS INVESTOR DECISIONS

Investing is a difficult process. It entails gathering information, analyzing the information, and making a decision based on that information. However, overconfidence causes us to misinterpret the accuracy of our information and overestimate our skill in analyzing it. This can lead to poor investment decisions, which often manifest themselves as excessive trading, risk taking, and ultimately portfolio losses.

Overconfident investors trade too much. Their overconfidence increases the amount they trade because it causes them to be too certain about their opinions. Investors' opinions derive from their beliefs regarding the accuracy of the information they have obtained and their ability to interpret it. In general, investors overestimate the precision of their information and are biased in their interpretation of that information.[4] Overconfident investors believe more strongly in their own valuation of a stock and concern themselves less about the beliefs of others.

Psychologists have found that men are more overconfident than women in tasks perceived to fall into the masculine domain, such as managing finances.[5] Men generally are more overconfident about their ability to make investment decisions than women are; therefore, male investors trade more frequently than female investors do.

Two financial economists, Brad Barber and Terrance Odean, examined the trading behavior of nearly 38,000 households through a large discount brokerage firm between 1991 and 1997.[6] They examined the level of trading in brokerage accounts owned by single and married men and women. A common measure for the level of trading is called *turnover*. Turnover is the percentage of stocks in the portfolio that changed during the year. For example, a 50 percent turnover during a year is the equivalent of an investor selling half the stocks in a portfolio during that year and purchasing new stocks. Similarly, a 200 percent turnover is equivalent to an investor selling all the stocks in the portfolio to purchase others, then selling those stocks to purchase a third set during one year's time.

The study shows that single men trade the most. As illustrated in Figure 2.1, single men trade at a rate equivalent to an 85 percent annual turnover. This compares with an annual turnover of 73 percent for married men. Married and single women trade only the equivalent of 53 percent and 51 percent in annual turnover, respectively. Note that this is consistent with overconfidence; that is, male

FIGURE 2.1 Annual Portfolio Turnover by Gender and Marital Status

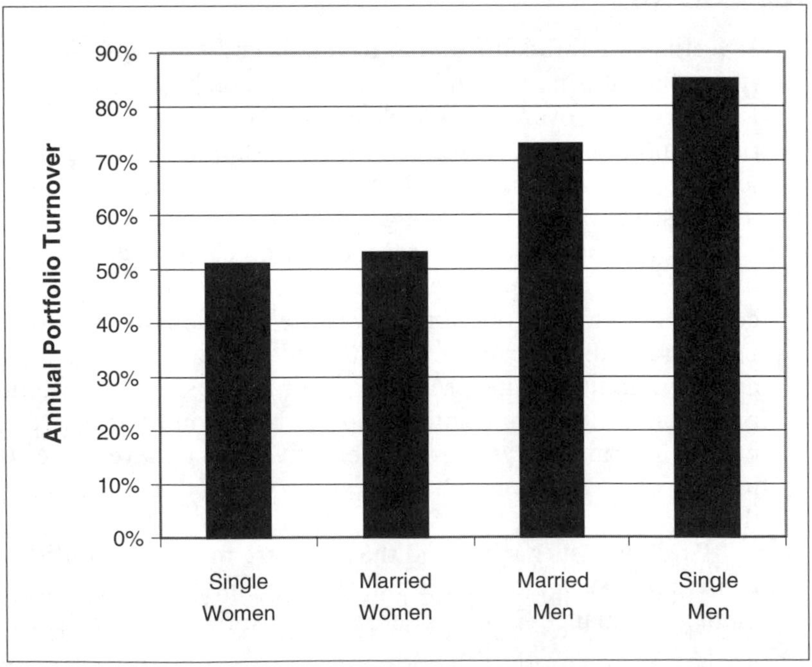

investors are more overconfident than female investors, leading to higher levels of trading.

On the other hand, it is possible that men are not overconfident, but rather that they might be better informed. If you truly have better information, trading on that information should lead to achieving higher returns.

In general, overconfident investors trade more, but is higher turnover and increased trading bad? Barber and Odean also explore this issue.[7] In a sample of 78,000 household accounts over the period 1991 to 1996, they examined the relationship between turnover and portfolio returns. Consider an investor who receives accurate information and is highly capable of interpreting it. The investor's high frequency of trading should result in high returns due to the individual's skill and the quality of the information. In fact, these returns should be high enough to beat a simple buy-and-hold strategy while covering the costs of trading. On the other hand, if the investor does not have superior ability but rather is suffering from a dose of overconfidence, then the high frequency of turnover will not result in portfolio returns large enough to beat the buy-and-hold strategy and cover costs.

First, Barber and Odean determined the level of trading for the investors in their sample and categorized them into five groups. The first 20 percent of investors having the lowest turnover rate were placed in the first group. On average, this group turned over their portfolio at a rate of 2.4 percent per year. The 20 percent of investors with the next-lowest turnover rate were placed in the second group. This process continued until the investors with the highest turnover rate were placed in the fifth (and last) group. This high-turnover rate group experienced an average annual turnover rate of more than 250 percent per year.

Figure 2.2 reports the average annual return for each of the five groups. Note that all five groups earned the same 18.7 percent annually in gross returns. Therefore, high-turnover investors did not realize higher returns for their additional efforts. However, commissions must be paid for buying and selling stocks. This has a greater effect on the investors who trade more frequently, as illustrated in the figure. Net returns (returns after commission costs) to the investor are much lower for the high-turnover group. The net returns for the lowest-turnover group average 18.5 percent per year, versus 11.4 percent for the highest-turnover group.

The net difference of 7 percent per year between the highest- and lowest-turnover groups is dramatic. For example, if the investors in the lowest-turnover group invest $10,000 over 5 years, earning

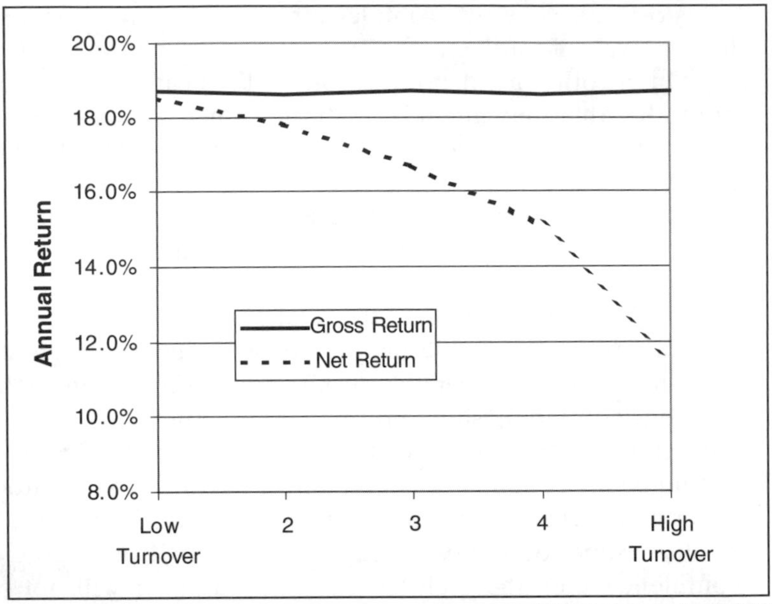

FIGURE 2.2 Annual Return of Investors Sorted by Portfolio Turnover

18.5 percent per year, they will have $23,366. If the investors in the highest-turnover group invest the same amount and receive 11.4 percent per year, they can expect only $17,156—a difference of more than $5,000. Overconfidence-based trading is hazardous when it comes to accumulating wealth.

High commission costs are not the only problem caused by excessive trading. It has been observed that overconfidence leads to trading too frequently, as well as to purchasing the wrong stocks. Barber and Odean limited their analysis to a sample of brokerage accounts that had complete liquidations of a stock followed by the purchase of a different stock within 3 weeks. Then they followed the performance of the stocks sold and purchased over the subsequent 4 months and 1 year.

They wanted to determine whether selling stock A and purchasing stock B typically was a good decision. Apparently not. The stocks that investors sold earned 2.6 percent during the following 4 months, whereas the replacement stocks earned only 0.11 percent. In the year following the trades, stocks that had been sold outperformed stocks purchased by 5.8 percent.[8] Not only does overconfidence cause you to trade too much and burn money on commissions, it can also cause you to sell a good-performing stock in order to purchase a poorer one.

OVERCONFIDENCE AND RISK

Overconfidence also affects investors' risk-taking behavior. Rational investors try to maximize returns while minimizing the amount of risk taken. However, overconfident investors misinterpret the level of risk they take. After all, if an investor is confident that the stocks picked will have a high return, then where is the risk?

The portfolios of overconfident investors will have higher risk for two reasons. First is the tendency to purchase higher-risk stocks. Higher-risk stocks are generally from smaller, newer companies. The second reason is a tendency to underdiversify their portfolio.

Prevalent risk can be measured in several ways: portfolio volatility, beta, and the size of the firms in the portfolio. Portfolio volatility measures the degree of ups and downs the portfolio experiences. High-volatility portfolios exhibit dramatic swings in price and are indicative of underdiversification. Beta is a variable commonly used in the investment industry to measure the riskiness of a security. It measures the degree a portfolio changes with the stock market. A beta of 1 indicates that the portfolio closely follows the market. A higher beta indicates that the security has higher risk and will exhibit more volatility than the stock market in general.

The series of studies by Barber and Odean show that overconfident investors take more risk. They found that single men have the highest-risk portfolios followed by married men, married women, and single women. That is, the portfolios of single men have the highest volatility and the highest beta, and tend to include the stocks of smaller companies. For the five groups of investors sorted by turnover, the high-turnover group invested in stocks of smaller firms with higher betas compared with the stocks of the low-turnover group. Overall, overconfident investors perceive their actions to be less risky than generally proves to be the case.

ILLUSION OF KNOWLEDGE

Where does overconfidence come from? It comes partially from the illusion of knowledge. This refers to the tendency for people to believe that the accuracy of their forecasts increases with more information; that is, more information increases one's knowledge about something and improves one's decisions.[9]

However, this is not always the case. For example, if I roll a fair, six-sided die, what number do you think will come up, and how sure are you that you are right? Clearly, you can pick any number between 1 and 6 and have a one-sixth chance of being right. Now let me tell you that the last three rolls of the die have each produced the number 4. I will roll the die again. What number do you think will come up, and what is your chance of being right? If the die is truly fair, then you could still pick any number between 1 and 6 and have a one-sixth chance of being correct. The added information does not increase your ability to forecast the roll of the die. However, many people believe the number 4 has a greater chance (more than one sixth) of being rolled again. Others believe the number 4 has a lower chance of being rolled again. These people think their chance of being right is higher than reality. That is, the new information makes people more confident in their predictions even though their chances for being correct do not change.

Using the Internet, investors have access to vast quantities of information. This information includes historical data such as past prices, returns, and firm operational performance, as well as current information such as real-time news, prices, and volume. Information access for individual investors on the Internet is nearly as good as that of professional investors. However, most individual investors lack the training and experience of professional investors and therefore are less sure of how to interpret the information; that is, this information does not give them as much knowledge about the situation as they think because they do not have the training to interpret it properly.

Many individual investors realize they have a limited ability to interpret investment information, so they use the Internet for help. Investors can get analyst recommendations, subscribe to expert services, join newsgroups, and learn others' opinions through chat rooms and Web postings. However, online investors need to take what they see in these chat rooms with a grain of salt. Not all recommendations are from experts.

In fact, few of them may be. A recent study examines the stocks recommended by messages posted on the boards of two Internet newsgroups.[10] Most of the stocks recommended had recently performed very well or very poorly. The stocks with very good performance the previous month were recommended as a purchase (momentum strategy). These stocks subsequently underperformed the market by more than 19 percent the next month. The stocks that were recommended for purchase with extremely poor performance during the previous month (value strategy) outperformed the market by more than 25 percent over the following month. Overall, the stocks recommended for purchase did not perform significantly different than the market in general.

Another study finds that positive message board postings at RagingBull.com are not associated with positive stock returns the following day or week.[11] However, unusually high numbers of postings are associated with higher trading volume. These studies conclude that message board stock recommendations do not contain valuable information for investors. However, if investors perceive the messages as having increased their knowledge, they might be overconfident about their investment decisions. The higher trading volume indicates that this might be the case.

ILLUSION OF CONTROL

Another important psychological factor is the illusion of control. People often believe they have influence over the outcome of uncontrollable events. The key attributes that foster the illusion of control are choice, outcome sequence, task familiarity, information, and active involvement.[12] Online investors can routinely experience these attributes.

Choice

Making an active choice induces control. For example, people who choose their own lottery numbers believe they have a better chance of winning than people who have numbers given to them at random. Because online brokers do not give investors advice, investors must make their own choices regarding what (and when) to buy and sell.

Outcome Sequence

The way in which an outcome occurs affects the illusion of control. Early positive outcomes give the person a greater illusion of control than early negative outcomes do. Investors were getting on the Web during the late 1990s and taking control of their investments, and because this period was an extended bull market interval, they likely experienced many positive outcomes.

Task Familiarity

The more familiar people are with a task, the more they feel in control of the task. As discussed later in this chapter, investors have been becoming familiar with the online investment environment and have been active traders and participants in Web information services.

Information

When a greater amount of information is obtained, the illusion of control is greater, as well. The vast amount of information on the Internet already has been illustrated.

Active Involvement

When a person participates a great deal in a task, the feeling of being in control is also proportionately greater. Online investors have high participation rates in the investment process. Investors using discount brokers (such as online brokers) must conduct their own investment decision-making process. These investors obtain and evaluate information, make trading decisions, and place the trades.

The Internet fosters further active involvement by providing the medium for investment chat rooms, message boards, and newsgroups. Internet investment services firms such as Yahoo!, Motley Fool, Silicon Investor, and The Raging Bull sponsor message boards on their Web sites where investors can communicate with each other. Typically, message boards are available for each stock listed on the exchange. Users post a message about the firm using an alias or simply read the message postings.

Past Successes

Overconfidence is learned through past success. If a decision turns out to be good, it is attributed to skill and ability. If a decision turns out to be bad, then it is attributed to bad luck. The more successes people experience, the more they will attribute it to their own ability, even when much luck is involved.

During bull markets, individual investors will attribute too much of their success to their own abilities, which makes them overconfident. As a consequence, overconfident behaviors (e.g., high levels of trading and risk taking) will be more pronounced in bull markets than in bear markets.[13]

This is borne out in the behavior of investors during the bull market of the late 1990s and the subsequent bear market. As the bull market raged on, individual investors traded more than ever. In addition, investors allocated higher proportions of their assets to stocks, invested in riskier companies, and even leveraged their positions by using more margin (borrowed money).[14] These behaviors slowly became reversed as the overconfidence of the bull market faded and the bear market dragged on.

ONLINE TRADING

Brad Barber and Terry Odean investigated the trading behavior of 1,607 investors who switched from a phone-based trading system to an Internet-based trading system at a discount brokerage firm.[15] In the 2 years prior to the time investors went online, the average portfolio turnover was about 70 percent. After going online, the trading of these investors immediately jumped to a turnover of 120 percent. Some of this increase is transitory; however, the turnover rate of these investors is still 90 percent 2 years after going online.

A different study investigated the effect of Web-based trading in 401(k) pension plans.[16] A total of 100,000 plan participants from two companies were given the opportunity to trade their 401(k) assets using an Internet service. The advantage of studying these trades is that because they occurred within a qualified pension plan, liquidity needs and tax-loss selling were not factors. All trades can be considered speculative. Their conclusions were consistent with overconfident trading; specifically, they found that trading frequency doubled and portfolio turnover increased by 50 percent.

ONLINE TRADING AND PERFORMANCE

Barber and Odean also examined the performance of the investors before and after going online. Before switching to the online trading service, these investors were successful. As illustrated in Figure 2.3, they earned nearly 18 percent per year before going online. This represents a return of 2.35 percent more than the general stock market. However, after going online, these investors experienced reduced returns. Thcy averaged annual returns of only 12 percent, underperforming the market by 3.5 percent.

The successful performance of these investors before going online might have fostered overconfidence due to the illusion of control (via the outcome sequence). This overconfidence might have caused them to choose the Internet trading service. Unfortunately, the Internet trading environment exacerbates the overconfidence problem, inducing excessive trading. Ultimately, investor returns are reduced.

To summarize this chapter, individual investors can be overconfident about their abilities, knowledge, and future prospects. Overconfidence leads to excessive trading, which lowers portfolio returns. The lower returns result from the commission costs associated with high levels of trading and the propensity to purchase stocks that underperform the stocks that were sold. Overconfidence also leads to greater risk taking due to underdiversification and a focus on investing in small companies with higher betas. Last, the trend of using online brokerage accounts is making investors more overconfident than ever before.

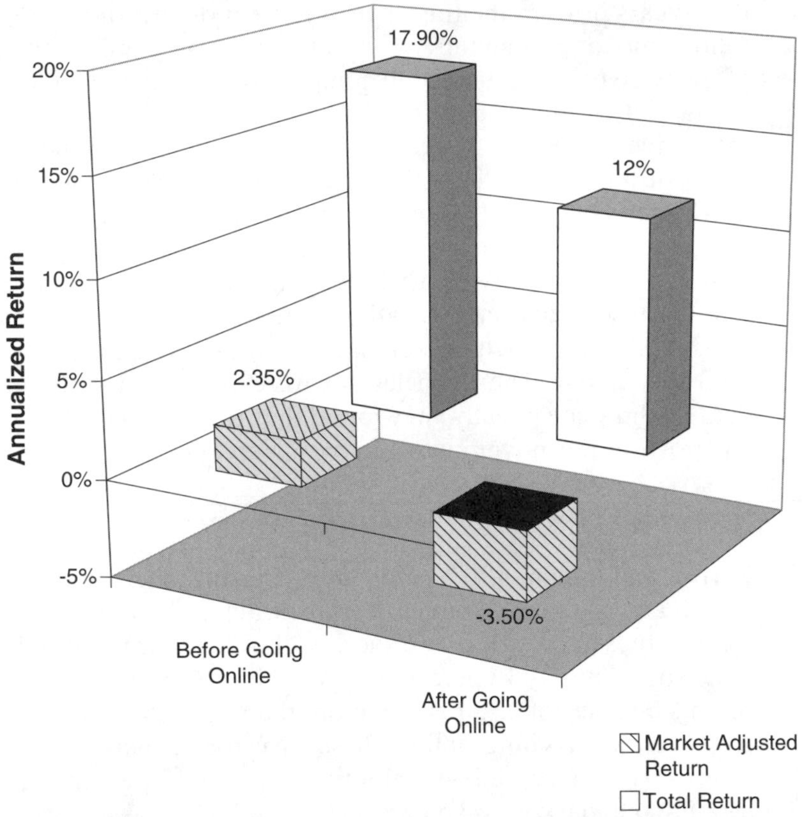

FIGURE 2.3 Annualized Market Adjusted Return and Total Return of Investors Before and After Switching to an Online Trading System

Questions

1. Would you expect investors to be more overconfident in the midst of a bull market or a bear market? Why?
2. How might an investor's portfolio have changed from 1995 to 2000 if the investor had become overconfident? Give examples of the numbers and types of stocks in the portfolio.
3. How does the Internet "trick" investors into believing they have wisdom?
4. How might using an online broker (versus a full-service broker) create an illusion of control?

End Notes

1. Ola Svenson, "Are We All Less Risky and More Skillful than Our Fellow Drivers?" *Acta Psychologica* 47(1981): 143–148.
2. Arnold C. Cooper, Carolyn Y. Woo, and William C. Dunkelberg, "Entrepreneurs' Perceived Chances for Success," *Journal of Business Venturing* 3(1988): 97–108.

3. E. J. Langer, "The Illusion of Control," *Journal of Personality and Social Psychology* 32(1975): 311–328.
4. Brad Barber and Terrance Odean, "The Courage of Misguided Convictions," *Financial Analysts Journal* (Nov./Dec. 1999): 41–55.
5. Sylvia Beyer and Edward Bowden, "Gender Differences in Self-Perceptions: Convergent Evidence from Three Measures of Accuracy and Bias," *Journal of Personality and Social Psychology* 59(1997): 960–970. See also Melvin Prince, "Women, Men, and Money Styles," *Journal of Economic Psychology* 14(1993): 175–182.
6. Brad Barber and Terrance Odean, "Boys Will Be Boys: Gender, Overconfidence, and Common Stock Investment," *Quarterly Journal of Economics* 116(2001): 261–292.
7. Brad Barber and Terrance Odean, "Trading Is Hazardous to Your Wealth: The Common Stock Investment Performance of Individual Investors," *Journal of Finance* 55(2000): 773–806.
8. Terrance Odean, "Do Investors Trade Too Much?" *American Economic Review* 89(1999): 1279–1298.
9. For a discussion and test of the illusion of knowledge, see Dane Peterson and Gordon Pitz, "Confidence, Uncertainty, and the Use of Information," *Journal of Experimental Psychology* 14(1988): 85–92.
10. Michael Dewally, "Internet Investment Advice: Investing with a Rock of Salt," *Financial Analysts Journal* 59(July/August 2003): 65–77.
11. Robert Tumarkin and Robert F. Whitelaw, "News or Noise? Internet Postings and Stock Prices," *Financial Analysts Journal* (May/June 2001): 41–51.
12. Paul Presson and Victor Benassi, "Illusion of Control: A Meta-Analytic Review," *Journal of Social Behavior and Personality* 11(1996): 493–510.
13. Simon Gervais and Terrance Odean, "Learning to Be Overconfident," *Review of Financial Studies* 14(2001): 1–27. Also see Kent Daniel, David Hirshleifer, and Avanidhar Subrahmanyam, "Overconfidence, Arbitrage, and Equilibrium Asset Pricing," *Journal of Finance* 56(2001): 921–965.
14. Brad Barber and Terrance Odean, "The Internet and the Investor," *Journal of Economic Perspectives* 15(2001): 41–54.
15. Brad Barber and Terrance Odean, "Online Investors: Do the Slow Die First?" *Review of Financial Studies* 15(2002): 455–487.
16. James Choi, David Laibson, and Andrew Metrick, "How Does the Internet Increase Trading? Evidence from Investor Behavior in 401(k) Plans," *Journal of Financial Economics* 64(2002): 397–421.

CHAPTER 3

Pride and Regret

People avoid actions that create regret and seek actions that cause pride. Regret is the emotional pain that comes with realizing that a previous decision turned out to be a bad one. Pride is the emotional joy of realizing that a decision turned out well.

Consider this state lottery example.[1] You have been selecting the same lottery ticket numbers every week for months. Not surprisingly, you have not won. A friend suggests a different set of numbers. Do you change numbers?

Clearly, the likelihood of the old set of numbers winning is the same as the likelihood of the new set of numbers winning. This example has two possible sources of regret. Regret will result if you stick with the old numbers and the new numbers win. This is called the regret of omission (not taking an action). Regret also will result if you switch to the new numbers and the old numbers win. The regret of an action you took is the regret of commission. In which case would the pain of regret be stronger? The stronger regret would most likely result from switching to the new numbers because you have a lot of emotional capital in the old numbers—after all, you have been selecting them for months. A regret of commission generally is more painful than a regret of omission.

DISPOSITION EFFECT

Avoiding regret and seeking pride affects people's behavior, but how does it affect investment decisions? Two financial economists, Hersh Shefrin and Meir Statman, adapted this psychological behavior to the investor.[2] They show that fearing regret and seeking pride causes investors to be predisposed to selling winners too early and riding losers too long. They call this the disposition effect.

Consider the situation in which you wish to invest in a particular stock. However, you have no cash and must sell a position in another stock in order to have the cash for the new purchase. You can sell either of two stocks you hold. Stock A has earned a 20 percent return since you purchased it, whereas stock B has lost 20 percent. Which stock do you sell? Selling stock A validates your good decision to purchase it in the first place. It would make you feel proud to lock in your profit. Selling stock B at a loss means realizing that your decision to purchase it was bad. You would feel the pain of regret. The disposition effect predicts that you will sell the winner, stock A. Selling stock A triggers the feeling of pride and allows you to avoid regret.

DISPOSITION EFFECT AND WEALTH

Why is it a problem that investors may sell their winners more frequently than their losers? One reason relates to the U.S. tax code. The taxation of capital gains causes the selling of losers to be the wealth-maximizing strategy. Selling a winner leads to the realization of a capital gain, and hence payment of taxes. Those taxes reduce your profit. On the other hand, selling the losers gives you a chance to reduce your taxes, thus decreasing the amount of the loss. Reconsider the aforementioned example and assume that capital gains are taxed at the 20 percent rate (Table 3.1). If your positions in stocks A and B are each valued at $1,000, then the original purchase price of stock A must have been $833, and the purchase price of stock B must have been $1,250.

If you sell stock A, you receive $1,000 but pay taxes of $33, so your net proceeds are $967. Alternatively, you could sell stock B and receive $1,000 plus gain a tax credit of $50 to be used against other capital gains, so your net proceeds are $1,050. If the tax rate is higher than 20 percent (as in the case of gains realized within 1 year of the stock purchase), then the advantage of selling the loser is even greater. Interestingly, the disposition effect predicts the selling of winners even though selling the losers is the wealth-maximizing strategy.

TABLE 3.1 Capital Gains and Taxation

Sell	*Stock A*	*Stock B*
Sale Proceeds	$1,000	$1,000
Tax Basis	$ 833	$1,250
Taxable Gain (loss)	$ 177	($ 250)
Tax (credit) at 20 Percent	$ 33	($ 50)
After-Tax Proceeds	$ 967	$1,050

...STS OF AVOIDING REGRET AND SEEKING PRIDE

Do investors behave in a rational manner by predominantly selling losers, or are investors affected by their psychology and have a tendency to sell their winners? Several studies provide evidence that investors behave in a manner more consistent with the disposition effect (selling winners). These studies generally fall into two categories: studies that examine the stock market and those that examine investor trades.

For example, Stephan Ferris, Robert Haugen, and Anil Makhija[3] examined the trading volume of stocks following price changes. If investors trade to maximize wealth, then they should sell stocks with price declines and capture the tax benefits. In addition, they should refrain from selling stocks with price gains to avoid paying taxes. Therefore, the volume of trades should be high for stocks with losses and low for stocks with gains. Alternatively, investors may opt to avoid regret and seek pride. In this case, it would be expected that investors will hold their losers and sell their winners. Therefore, high volume in the stocks with gains and low volume in the stocks with declines is consistent with the disposition effect.

Ferris and associates used a methodology that determines the normal level of volume expected for each stock. They reported results that can be interpreted as a form of abnormal volume; that is, a negative abnormal volume indicates less trading than normal, whereas a positive abnormal volume indicates more trading than normal. Using the 30 smallest stocks on the New York Stock Exchange (NYSE) and the American Stock Exchange (AMEX) during December 1981 to January 1985, they grouped each stock into categories based on the percentage gain or loss at each point in time. The results are presented in Figure 3.1.

Note that the stocks with losses of more than 22.5 percent are grouped in the left column. The loss diminishes in each column to the right until the middle of the graph, where stocks had small losses or gains. Stocks in the far-right column had a gain of more than 22.5 percent. In general, stocks with gains had positive abnormal volume, whereas stocks with declines had negative abnormal volume. Higher volume in stocks with gains and lower volume in stocks with declines is consistent with the disposition effect.

This analysis was performed separately for volume in December and the rest of the year, because people are more aware of the benefits of selling losers and gaining tax advantages in December. Therefore, it would seem that investors might be more likely to enact a

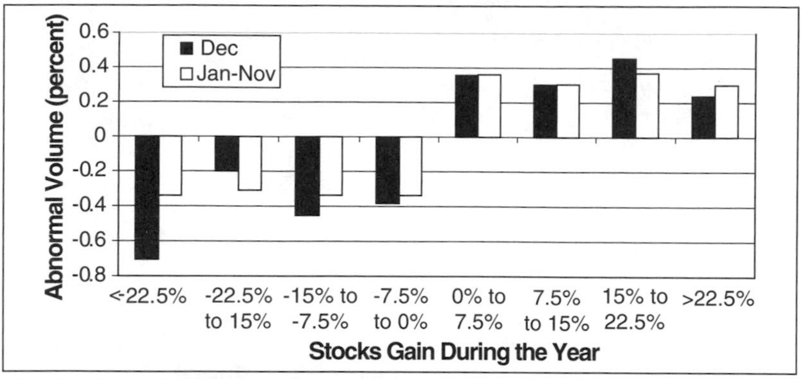

FIGURE 3.1 Volume of Stocks After Losses and Gains

wealth-maximizing strategy in December versus the other months. However, Figure 3.1 shows that investors avoid regret and seek pride as much in December as during the rest of the year.

Other studies have analyzed the actual trades and portfolios of individual investors. In an older study using trades from a national brokerage house during 1964 to 1970, Schlarbaum and associates. examined 75,000 round-trip trades.[4] A round-trip trade is a stock purchase followed later by the sale of the stock.

They examined the length of time the stock was held and the return that was received. Are investors quick to close out a position when it has taken a loss or when it has a gain? Consider the behavior implied by the disposition effect. If you buy a stock that goes up quickly, you will be more inclined to sell it quickly. If you buy a stock that goes down or remains level you are more inclined to hold while waiting for it to go up. Therefore, stocks held for a short time tend to be winners and stocks held longer are likely to be less successful. Figure 3.2 shows the average annualized return for a position held for less than 1 month, 1 to 6 months, 6 to 12 months, and more than 1 year. The figure indicates that investors are quick to realize their gains. The average annualized return for stocks purchased then sold within 1 month was 45 percent. The returns for stocks held 1 to 6 months, 6 to 12 months, and more than 1 year were 7.8 percent, 5.1 percent, and 4.5 percent, respectively. It appears that investors are quick to sell winners.

Using a more recent sample, Terrance Odean studied the trades of 10,000 trading accounts from a nationwide discount brokerage during 1987 to 1993.[5] At each sell trade, Odean calculated the amount of gains and losses the investor had on paper in his or her portfolio.

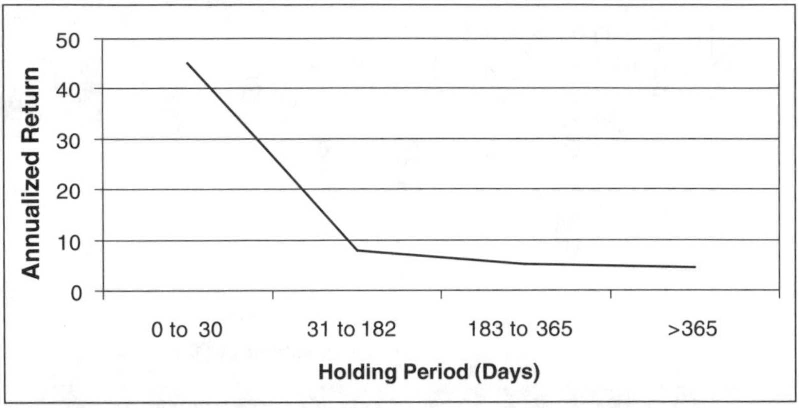

FIGURE 3.2 Annualized Return for Different Investor Holding Periods

If the investor sold a winner, then he calculated the gain on the stock and divided by the total paper gains available to the investor. The result is the proportion of total gains that the investor realized with the sell trade. If the stock sold was a loser, then the proportion of total losses realized was computed.

Odean found that when investors sell winners, the sale represents 23 percent of the total gains of the investor's portfolio. Alternatively, when a loser is sold, it represents only 15.5 percent of the unrealized losses in the portfolio. On average, investors are 50 percent more likely to sell a winner than a loser.

As a further test of the disposition effect, Mark Grinblatt and Matti Keloharju studied all investor trades in Finland during 1995 and 1996.[6] They found that a large positive return the previous week significantly increases an investor's propensity to sell the stock. Interestingly, this is true for all levels of investor sophistication (individual investors and different groups of institutional investors). On the other hand, a large decrease in price significantly increases the probability that the investor will hold the stock. They also found that the more recently the stock gains or losses occurred (last week versus last month), the stronger the propensity was to sell winners and hold losers.

THE MARKET FOR HOUSES

As another example of the aversion to sell losers, consider the housing market. Like the stock market, real estate prices experience bull and bear markets. Over a several-year period, home owners might see the value of their home dramatically increase or decrease. For example, between 1982 and 1989, housing prices in Boston increased by about 170 percent. The prices then decreased by 40 percent over the next 4 years.

If you purchased a home near the market peak and wished to sell it a few years later after the decline, you would be looking at a potential loss. Because of loss aversion, home owners might be unwilling to accept market prices for their houses in a down market. Consider two types of home sellers in a down market. One seller purchased the house many years ago and can still make a profit at current market prices. The other seller purchased the home just before the decline in prices and must sell at a loss to sell the home. This seller faces the pain of regret.

A study of the Boston housing market shows that the seller facing a loss tends to list the property at a 25 percent to 35 percent premium over the expected selling price. The seller who is not facing regret can set a more realistic price. The higher listing price by the sellers who are facing losses also leads to a longer time on the market before accepting an offer.[7]

SELLING WINNERS TOO SOON AND HOLDING LOSERS TOO LONG

The disposition effect not only predicts the selling of winners, it suggests that the winners are sold too soon and the losers are held too long. What does selling too soon or holding too long imply for investors? Selling winners too soon suggests that those stocks will continue to perform well after they are sold. Holding losers too long suggests that those stocks with price declines will continue to perform poorly.

When an investor sold a winning stock, Odean found that the stock generally beat the market during the next year by an average 2.35 percent.[8] During this same year, the loser stocks that the investors kept generally underperformed the market by −1.06 percent. Investors tend to sell the stock that ends up providing a high return and keep the stock that provides a low return.

Note that the fear of regret and the seeking of pride hurt investors' wealth in two ways. First, investors are paying more in taxes because of the disposition to sell winners instead of losers. Second, investors earn a lower return on their portfolio because they sell the winners too early and hold poorly performing stocks that continue to perform poorly.

Martin Weber and Colin Camerer designed a stock trading experiment for their students.[9] They create six "stocks" for trading and show the students the last three price points of each stock. They designed the experiment so that the stock prices are likely to trend; that is, stocks with gains will likely continue to gain, whereas stocks with declines will likely continue to decline. The students are shown the potential prices for each stock in the future. Because of this experimental design, stocks with losses should be sold and stocks with gains should be held (the opposite of the disposition effect). Contrary to the wealth-maximizing strategy, the subjects sold fewer shares when the price was below the purchase price than when the price was above, thus exhibiting the disposition effect.

DISPOSITION EFFECT AND NEWS

One study investigated all the trades of individual investors in 144 New York Stock Exchange firms during the November 1990 through January 1991 period.[10] Specifically, how investors react to news about the company and news about the economy was studied. News about a company primarily affects the price of the company's stock, whereas economic news affects all firms. Good news about a firm that increases the stock price induces investors to sell (selling winners). Bad news about a firm does not induce investors to sell (holding losers). This is consistent with avoiding regret and seeking pride.

However, news about the economy does not induce investor trading. Although good economic news increases stock prices and bad economic news lowers stock prices, this does not cause individual investors to sell. In fact, investors are less likely than usual to sell winners after good economic news. These results are not consistent with the disposition effect.

This illustrates an interesting characteristic of regret. When taking a stock loss, investors feel stronger regret if the loss can be tied to their own decision. However, if investors can attribute the loss to reasons that are out of their control, then the feeling of regret is weaker.[11] For example, if the stock you hold declines in price when the stock market itself is advancing, then you have made a bad choice and regret is strong. However, if the stock you hold declines in price during a general market decline, then this is essentially out of your control, so the feeling of regret is weak.

Investor actions are consistent with the disposition effect for company news because the feeling of regret is strong. In the case of economic news, investors have a weaker feeling of regret because the outcome is considered beyond their control. This leads to actions that are not consistent with the predictions of the disposition effect.

REFERENCE POINTS

The pleasure of achieving gains and the pain of losses is a powerful motivator of human behavior. However, it might be difficult to determine whether some investment transactions are considered a profit or a loss. For example, Bob purchases a stock for $50 per share. At the end of the year, the stock is trading for $100. Also at end of the year, Bob re-examines his investment positions in order to record and determine his net worth and monitor the progress he has made toward his financial goals. Six months later, Bob sells the stock for $75 per share. He has made a profit of $25 per share. However, the profit is $25 per share lower than if he had sold at the end-of-year price. Clearly he made a $25 per-share profit. However, does Bob feel like he made a profit, or does he feel like he lost money?

This issue deals with a reference point. A reference point is the stock price that we compare with the current stock price. The current stock price is $75. Is the reference point the purchase price of $50 or the end-of-year price of $100? The brain's choice of a reference point is important because it determines whether we feel the pleasure of obtaining a profit or the pain of a loss.

The early investigations into the psychology of investors assumed that the purchase price was the reference point. However, investors monitor and remember their investment performance over the period of a year.[12] If the purchase was made long ago, then investors tend to use a more recently determined reference point.

What recent stock price is used as a reference? Possible recent references are the mean or median price of the past year. Additionally, the 52-week high and low prices are commonly reported in the media. Recent research suggests that investors use the 52-week maximum as the reference point.

An interesting investigation of the exercising of stock options illustrates the reference point.[13] Some managerial corporate employees receive stock options as part of their compensation. These options are frequently structured so that the strike price is equal to the price of the stock at the time the options are issued. The employee cannot exercise the options for a period of several years (the vesting period). Afterward, the employee can exercise the options and receive the difference between the stock price at the time and the strike price of the option.

Studying the employee option exercise has several advantages. First, employees who receive options as compensation are usually more sophisticated employees. Second, these options usually have a maturity date, and the employee knows that the options must be exercised before they expire. This feature helps mitigate any status quo bias. Third, a clear reference point does not exist. The options themselves have no price. The option strike price is an important reference because the stock price must be above the strike for any profit to be achieved. However, if the stock price is above the strike price after the vesting period, what reference point does the employee use?

It appears that the most likely reference point used is the highest price of the previous year. Using detailed records for 50,000 employees at seven corporations, Chip Heath, Steven Huddart, and Mark Lang found that the rate of exercising options nearly doubles when the stock price moves above the 52-week high. Consider the employees who want to exercise some options. The current stock price is lower than the 52-week high. Using this yearly high as a reference, the employees consider their position to be at a loss. Wanting to avoid regret, the employees wait until the stock price moves higher again so they can "break even." When the stock price meets or exceeds the 52-week high, the employees are much more likely to exercise the options because they believe the stock has exceeded the reference point. The researchers showed that the rate of option exercise increases when the stock price crosses a historical maximum.

In another study on option exercise, Allen Poteshman and Vitaly Serbin found that some investors irrationally exercise stock options early.[14] While exercising the options early fails to maximize wealth, this irrational behavior is triggered when the underlying stock price moves above its 52-week high price. Other possible reference points were investigated (75 percent, 50 percent, and 25 percent of the 52-week high), but it appears that the 52-week high is the most pervasively used by investors.

In the investor's mind, the reference point determines whether a position is at a profit or loss. However, it appears that investors periodically update the reference point to reflect unrealized profits. Returning to the example at the beginning of this section, Bob probably feels like he lost money because he moved his reference point to $100 when he recorded that price in his end-of-year evaluation.

To summarize this chapter, people act (or fail to act) to avoid regret and seek pride, which causes investors to sell their winners too soon and hold their losers too long. This behavior hurts investor wealth in two ways. First, investors pay more capital gains taxes because they sell winners. Second, investors earn a lower return because the winners they sell and no longer have continue to perform well, while the losers they still hold continue to perform poorly.

Questions

1. Consider an investor's statement: "If the stock price would only get back up to what I paid for it, I'd sell it!" Describe how the biases in this chapter are influencing the investor's decision.
2. How would the number of stocks held in the portfolio impact the disposition effect?
3. How can succumbing to the disposition effect harm wealth?

End Notes

1. This example is adapted from Roger G. Clarke, Stock Krase, and Meir Statman, "Tracking Errors, Regret, and Tactical Asset Allocation," *Journal of Portfolio Management* 20(1994): 16–24.
2. Hersh Shefrin and Meir Statman, "The Disposition to Sell Winners Too Early and Ride Losers Too Long: Theory and Evidence," *Journal of Finance* 40(1985): 777–790.
3. Stephen P. Ferris, Robert A. Haugen, and Anil K. Makhija, "Predicting Contemporary Volume with Historic Volume at Differential Price Levels: Evidence Supporting the Disposition Effect," *Journal of Finance* 43(1988): 677–697.
4. Gary G. Schlarbaum, Wilbur G. Lewellen, and Ronald C. Lease, "Realized Returns on Common Stock Investments: The Experience of Individual Investors," *Journal of Business* 51(1978): 299–325.
5. Terrance Odean, "Are Investors Reluctant to Realize Their Losses?" *Journal of Finance* 53(1998): 1775–1798.
6. Mark Grinblatt and Matti Keloharju, "What Makes Investors Trade?" *Journal of Finance* 56(2001): 589–616.
7. This discussion is from David Genesove and Christopher Mayer, "Loss Aversion and Seller Behavior: Evidence from the Housing Market," *Quarterly Journal of Economics* 116(2001): 1233–1260.
8. Actually, Odean calculates an abnormal return that is not based on the market, but rather on matching firms.
9. Martin Weber and Colin F. Camerer, "The Disposition Effect in Securities Trading: An Experimental Analysis," *Journal of Economic Behavior & Organization* 33(1998): 167–184.
10. John R. Nofsinger, "The Impact of Public Information on Investors," *Journal of Banking and Finance* 25(2001): 1339–1366.
11. This discussion is adapted from Roger G. Clarke, Stock Krase, and Meir Statman, "Tracking Errors, Regret, and Tactical Asset Allocation," *Journal of Portfolio Management* 20(1994): 19.

12. Shlomo Benartzi and Richard Thaler, "Myopic Loss-Aversion and the Equity Premium Puzzle," *Quarterly Journal of Economics* 110(1995): 75–92.
13. This discussion derives from Chip Heath, Steven Huddart, and Mark Lang, "Psychological Factors and Stock Option Exercise," *Quarterly Journal of Economics* 114(1999): 601–627.
14. Allen Poteshman and Vitaly Serbin, "Clearly Irrational Financial Market Behavior: Evidence from the Early Exercise of Exchange Traded Stock Options," *Journal of Finance* 58(2003): 37–70.

CHAPTER 4

Considering the Past

A person who has not made peace with his losses is likely to accept gambles that would be unacceptable to him otherwise.

KAHNEMAN AND TVERSKY[1]

Consider this wager on a coin toss: Heads you win $20, tails you lose $20. Would you take this gamble? By the way, you won $100 earlier. Now would you take this gamble? Did your answer change after finding out that you had won earlier? What if you had lost $20 earlier? Would this make the gamble look any different to you?

Many people will take the gamble in one situation but not in another. The odds of winning the $20 do not change in the different scenarios, so the expected value of the gamble remains the same. Neither the risk nor the reward of the gamble changes between situations; therefore, people's reaction to risk must change.

People seem to use a past outcome as a factor in evaluating a current risky decision. In short, people are willing to take more risk after earning gains and less risk after losses. To illustrate this behavior, Richard Thaler and Eric Johnson asked 95 undergraduate economics students to take a series of two-step gambles using real money.[2] In the first step, money was either given or taken from the student. In the second step, the student was asked whether he or she wished to take the gamble presented. Their findings suggest a "house-money effect," a risk-aversion (or snake-bite) effect, and a "trying-to-break-even effect," which are discussed in the following sections.

HOUSE-MONEY EFFECT

After people have experienced a gain or profit, they are willing to take more risk. Gamblers refer to this feeling as playing with the house's money. After winning a big sum, amateur gamblers don't fully consider the new money as their own. Are you willing to take more risk with your opponent's money or your own money? Because gamblers don't fully integrate their winnings with their own money, they act like they are betting with the casino's money.

You have just won $15. Now you are faced with the opportunity to bet $4.50 on a coin toss. Do you place the bet? Seventy-seven percent of the economics students placed the bet. After just receiving their windfall of $15, most students were willing to take the risk. On the other hand, when students were asked to place a bet on a coin toss without receiving the $15, only 41 percent chose the gamble. Students are more willing to take a financial risk after a windfall profit even when not ordinarily inclined to take such a risk.

RISK-AVERSION (OR SNAKE-BITE) EFFECT

After experiencing a financial loss, people become less willing to take a risk. When faced with a gamble after already losing money, people generally choose to decline the gamble. Students who initially lost $7.50 were then asked to wager $2.25 on the flip of a coin. This time, the majority (60 percent) declined the gamble. After losing the initial money, the students might have felt "snake bit."

Snakes don't often bite people, but when it happens the person becomes more cautious. Likewise, after having been unlucky enough to lose money, people often feel they will continue to be unlucky; therefore, they avoid risk.

TRYING-TO-BREAK-EVEN EFFECT

Losers don't always avoid risk. People often jump at the chance to make up their losses. After having lost some money, a majority of the students accepted a "double-or-nothing" toss of the coin. In fact, a majority of the students were willing to accept a double-or-nothing toss of the coin even when they were told the coin was not "fair"; that is, students were willing to take a risk even though they knew they had less than a 50 percent chance of winning. The need for breaking even appears to be stronger than the snake-bite effect.

Another example of this break-even effect can be seen at the racetrack. After a day of betting on the horses and losing money, gamblers are more likely to bet on the long shots.[3] Odds of 15 to 1 mean that a $2 bet would win $30 if the horse wins. Of course, horses with odds of 15 to 1 are unlikely to win. The proportion of money bet on long shots is greater toward the end of the race day than at the beginning. It appears that gamblers are less likely to take this risk early in the day. However, those gamblers who have won money (house-money effect) or lost money (break-even effect) during the day are more likely to take this kind of risk. Winners take this risk because they feel as though they are playing with the house's money. Losers like the opportunity to break even without risking too much more. People without significant gains or losses prefer not to take the risk.

Consider the professional, full-time proprietary traders in the Treasury Bond futures contract at the Chicago Board of Trade. These traders take risk positions during the day and provide market-making services to earn a profit. All positions are usually closed out by the end of the day. With this single-day focus on profits, what do these traders do in the afternoon when they have lost money in the morning? Joshua Coval and Tyler Shumway examined the trades of 426 such traders in 1998.[4] They found that after losing money in the morning, the traders are more likely to increase their level of risk in the afternoon in an attempt to make back the losses. In addition, these traders are more likely to trade with other proprietary traders (instead of orders coming into the market from investors). These trades turn out to be, on average, losing trades. This illustrates the change in behavior that an investor might exhibit after experiencing a loss.

EFFECT ON INVESTORS

The house-money effect predicts that investors are more likely to purchase risky stocks after closing out a successful position. In other words, after locking in a gain by selling stock at a profit, investors are more likely to buy higher-risk stocks. Note that this behavior exacerbates the overconfidence behavior discussed in Chapter 2, because overconfident investors trade too much and buy higher-risk stocks.

The snake-bite effect also can affect investors. New or conservative investors might decide to "give the stock market a try." Adding some stocks to a portfolio gives the long-term investor better diversification and higher expected returns. However, if those stocks quickly decline in price, the first-time stock investor might feel snake bit. Consider the young investor who started by buying shares of a biotechnology company at $30 per share. Three days later, the stock declined to $28, and she panicked and sold the stock. Later the stock went up to $75, but she's "afraid to get back in the market."[5]

ENDOWMENT (OR STATUS QUO BIAS) EFFECTS

People often demand much more to sell an object than they would be willing to pay to buy it. This is known as the endowment effect.[6] A closely related behavior is people's tendency to keep what they have been given instead of exchanging it, known as status quo bias.[7]

Economists have examined the endowment effect by running experiments using their students. A common experiment is to give an object such as a university coffee mug to half the students in class. An ensuing market is created so those students with mugs who don't want them can sell them to students who want the mugs and don't have them. Traditional economic theory predicts that a market-clearing price will develop such that half the mugs will exchange hands. That is, half of the students who were given mugs will sell them to half of the students who did not receive a mug. However, in repeated experiments, students endowed with a mug typically demand twice the price that students without a mug are willing to pay. As a consequence, few mugs actually are traded. This finding occurs in experiments using different objects and using a repeating game, where students get experience trading in this type of market.[8]

What creates this endowment effect? Do people overestimate the value of the objects they own, or does parting with them cause too much pain? Consider the following experiment.[9] Students were asked to rank the attractiveness of six prizes. A less attractive prize, a pen, was given to half the students in the class. The other half of the class had a choice between the pen and two chocolate bars. Only 24 percent of the students picked the pen. The students who were originally given the pen were then given the opportunity to switch to the chocolate bars if they wanted. Even though most students ranked the chocolate higher than the pen as a prize, 56 percent of the students endowed with the pen elected not to switch. It does not appear that people overestimate the appeal of the object they own. Rather, they are more affected by the pain associated with giving up the object.

ENDOWMENT AND INVESTORS

How can endowment or status quo bias affect investors? People have a tendency to hold the investments they already have. For example, William Samuelson and Richard Zeckhauser told students to imagine that they just inherited a large sum of money. They can invest the money in different portfolios. Their choices are a moderate-risk company, a high-risk company, treasury bills, or municipal bonds.[10]

Many versions of this question were asked. In some versions, the subjects were told that the inheritance was already invested in the high-risk company. In other versions, the inheritance came in the form of the other investment options. Interestingly, the form of the investment at the time of endowment heavily influenced the portfolio choices made by the subjects. The high-risk company choice was more popular when the inheritance was already invested in the high-risk company. The same was true for the treasury bill. Clearly, the expected risk and return of portfolios dominated by treasury bills and high-risk companies are very different, yet subjects were more influenced by the status quo than by their own risk-and-return objectives.

The status quo bias increased as the number of investment options increased. That is, the more complicated the decision that was needed became, the more likely the subject was to choose to do nothing. In the real world, investors face the choice of investing in tens of thousands of company stocks, bonds, and mutual funds. All of these choices may overwhelm some investors. As a result, they often choose to avoid making a change. This can be a particular problem when the investments have lost money. Selling a loser would trigger regret (Chapter 3) and the pain of losing the endowment.

MEMORY AND DECISION MAKING

Memory is not as much a factual recording of events as it is a perception of the physical and emotional experience. This perception is affected by the way in which the events unfold. The process that records events in the brain can store different features of the experience. These stored features are the basis for subsequent recall.

Memory has an adaptive function: It determines whether a situation experienced in the past should be desired or avoided in the future. For example, if you remember an experience as having been worse than it really was, you would be excessively motivated to avoid similar experiences. Alternatively, if you remember an experience as better than it was, you will invest too much effort in seeking similar experiences. Therefore, inaccurate perceptions of past experiences can lead to poor decisions.

Experiments in psychology illustrate how memory works to affect decision making. Students experienced pain by putting their right hands in ice water (temperature of 14°C) for 60 seconds.[11]

Their left hands were then dipped into the water for 90 seconds. However, after the first 60 seconds at 14°C, the water temperature was increased to 15°C (unbeknownst to the subjects) for the final 30 seconds. Note that the left hand experienced the same level and duration of pain as the right hand. Then the left hand experienced 50 percent more duration of pain at a lower level. Which hand experienced more pain? Which experiment (short duration or long duration) would you endure if given the choice?

Seven minutes after dipping the second hand in the ice water, the students were given a choice of which experiment to repeat. Nearly 70 percent of the students chose to repeat the long trial.

Why did they choose the longer-duration pain experiment? The duration of experiences has little or no independent effect on the perception, or memory, of the pain experience. The most important factors of the pain experience are the peak pain and the level of pain at the end. The memory of the pain seems to be the average of the peak level of pain and the level of pain at the end of the experience.[12]

For the short trial, the peak level of pain and the pain at the end of the experiment were the same. However, because the temperature was increased at the end of the long trial (decreasing the pain), the end pain level was lower than the peak. The average between the peak and end levels of pain was, therefore, lower in the long trial than in the short trial. Consequently, students remembered the longer-duration trial as less painful, even though the longer trial started with the exact same level and duration of pain as the short trial but then added 50 percent more duration at a lower pain level.

In this experiment, a majority of the students chose to repeat a more painful experience because their memory failed to recall an accurate perception of the past experiences. In a similar experiment, researchers found that students' memories of the experience changed over time.[13] That is, the further the pain trials were in the past, the less painful the students remembered them to be.

MEMORY AND INVESTMENT DECISIONS

This phenomenon can affect investors, as well. The price pattern of a stock can affect how an investor makes decisions in the future. Consider this example of an investor purchasing two stocks. The investor buys the stock of a biotechnology firm and a pharmaceutical company. Each stock is purchased for $100. Throughout the following year, the price of the biotechnology stock slowly declines to $75. The price of the pharmaceutical stock stays at $100 until the very end of the year, when it plunges to $80.

For the year, the biotechnology stock performed worse than the pharmaceutical stock. However, the stocks lost money in different ways. The biotechnology stock experienced a gradual decline. The pharmaceutical stock experienced a dramatic loss at the end. The memory of the large loss at the end of the year is associated with a high degree of emotional pain. The memory of the slow loss provides less emotional pain. This can occur even though the biotechnology stock (the slow loser) performed worse. Therefore, when making decisions about these stocks for the following year, the investor might be overly pessimistic about the pharmaceutical stock.

This same pattern occurs for pleasurable experiences. People feel better about experiences with a high pleasure peak and end. Consider a scenario in which the two stocks increased in price. The biotechnology stock slowly increased to $125 over the year. The pharmaceutical stock rose dramatically to $120 at the end of the year. The memory of these events causes the investor to feel better about the pharmaceutical stock, even though it did not perform as well.

COGNITIVE DISSONANCE

Psychologists have studied specific consequences of memory problems. Consider that people typically view themselves as "smart and nice." Evidence that contradicts this image causes two seemingly opposite ideas. For example, suppose you want to think of yourself as nice, but the memory of one of your past actions suggests that you are not nice. Your brain would feel uncomfortable with this contradiction. Psychologists call this feeling *cognitive dissonance.* Simply stated, cognitive dissonance means that the brain is struggling with two opposite ideas—I am nice, but I am not nice. To avoid this psychological pain, people tend to ignore, reject, or minimize any information that conflicts with their positive self-image. Evidence that cannot be denied is accommodated by a change in beliefs.[14]

People's beliefs can change to be consistent with past decisions. We want to feel like we made the right decision. For example, racetrack gamblers were surveyed about the odds of "their horse" winning. Bettors just leaving the betting window gave their horse a better chance of winning than bettors standing in line to place their bets.[15]

Before placing the bet, gamblers feel more uncertainty about their chances. After placing the bet, their beliefs change to be consistent with their decision.

The avoidance of cognitive dissonance can affect the decision-making process in two ways. First, people can fail to make important decisions because it is too uncomfortable to contemplate the situation. For example, when considering the thought of saving for future retirement, some younger people may conjure an image of a feeble person with low earning power. To avoid the conflict between their good self-image and the contradictory future self-image, they avoid saving entirely. Second, the filtering of new information limits the ability to evaluate and monitor our investment decisions. If investors ignore negative information, how are they going to realize that an adjustment in their portfolio is necessary?

COGNITIVE DISSONANCE AND INVESTING

Investors seek to reduce psychological pain by adjusting their beliefs about the success of past investment choices. For example, at one point in time, an investor will make a decision to purchase a mutual fund. Over time, performance information about the fund will either validate or put into question the wisdom of picking that mutual fund. To reduce cognitive dissonance, the investor's brain will filter out or reduce the negative information and fixate on the positive information. Therefore, investor memory of past performance is better than actual past performance. In other words, you view yourself as a good investor, so the memory of your past investment performance adapts to be consistent with the self-image. You remember that you have done well, regardless of the actual performance.

William Goetzmann and Nadav Peles measured the recollections of investors.[16] They asked investors two questions about the return on their mutual fund investments during the previous year: (1) What was the return last year? (2) By how much did you beat the market? Note that these questions ask about actual performance and performance relative to possible alternatives. If investors are not biased by cognitive problems, then the average recollection of performance should be equal to the actual performance.

Goetzmann and Peles posed these questions to two groups of investors. The first group consisted of architects. Architects are highly educated professionals, but they might not be knowledgeable about investing. Twelve architects responded regarding 29 investments they

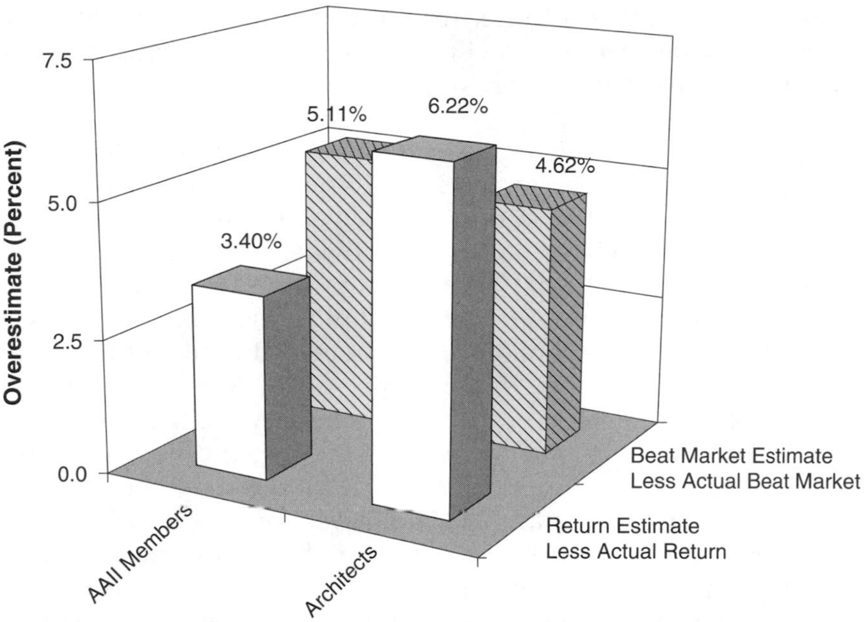

FIGURE 4.1 Errors in Memory (Cognitive Dissonance)

owned through their defined contribution pension plan. Figure 4.1 shows the architects' errors in their recollections. On average, they recalled an investment performance that was 6.22 percent higher than their actual return. They thought they did much better than they actually did.

It is difficult to outperform the market. Most stock mutual funds cannot consistently beat the Standard & Poor's 500 (S&P 500) Index. So how did the architects think they did? On average, their estimate of how much they beat the market was 4.62 percent too optimistic. This group of investors overestimated their actual return and overestimated their return relative to a benchmark.

Responses from a second group of investors were collected from members of a state chapter of the American Association of Individual Investors (AAII). The AAII is an association that provides education, information, and services to individual investors. Presumably, the members of the AAII are well educated in investing. Do these investors overestimate their past returns?

Twenty-nine AAII members responded concerning 57 mutual funds they owned. These investors overestimated their past returns by 3.40 percent, on average. They overestimated their performance relative to the market by 5.11 percent. Even though these people are educated investors, they are overly optimistic in recalling their past returns.

Also consider the responses of investors in a simulated market experiment.[17] The performance of 10 real mutual funds, a money market fund, and the S&P 500 Index over the 10-year period 1985 to 1994 were used in the simulation. Eighty master's-level business students allocated $100,000 to the investments as they wanted. Then 6-month returns are revealed to the investors, and they may re-allocate their portfolio. This was repeated until 20 turns of the game were completed. Note that throughout the experiment, the players saw the market return (as proxied by the S&P 500 Index) and their own portfolio holdings. After the game, the players were asked how they performed. What return did they get? Did they beat the market? On average, the players reported that they beat the market. This is a rosy perception of their performance because the group's average return was 8 percent below the market. When asked about their return, only 15 of the 80 were correct. A majority (47 out of 80) overestimated their total return.

People want to believe that their investment decisions are good. In the face of evidence to the contrary, the brain's defense mechanisms filter contradictory information and alter the recollection of the decision. It is hard to evaluate the progress toward investment goals or the need for an investment advisor objectively when the recollection of past performance is biased upward.

SUMMARY

Everyone has heard the investment advice "buy low, sell high." Why is this so hard to do in practice? One reason is that the house-money effect causes investors to seek riskier investments. This often manifests as the buying of stocks that have already had substantial increases in price. These stocks are risky because expectations have been elevated too much. In short, you buy high. If stock prices decline, you feel snake bit and you want out, so you sell low. The combination of the house-money and snake-bite effects causes you to do the opposite of buying low and selling high.

When many investors are affected by these problems, the entire market can be affected. The psychological bias of seeking (or ignoring) risk because of the house-money effect contributes to the creation of a price bubble. The psychological bias of avoiding risk in the snake-bite effect leads to stock prices that are driven too low after the bubble collapses.

Also, the human memory is more a recording of emotions and feelings of events than a recording of facts. This can cause investors to remember actual events inaccurately or even to ignore information that causes bad feelings.

Questions

1. Recently, television shows on poker have become popular on ESPN and the Travel Channel. The programs follow the action of no-limit Texas Hold'em tournaments. You might observe that after winning a big pot, many gamblers bet the next hand even when they have poor cards. After losing a big hand, many gamblers tend not to bet the next hand even when they have good cards. Explain these two behaviors.
2. Describe the appeal of "double-or-nothing" gambles. Be sure to include reference points (from Chapter 3).
3. Which impresses investors more: a steady change in price over time or a steady price followed by a dramatic change in price? Why?

End Notes

1. From Daniel Kahneman and Amos Tversky, "Prospect Theory: An Analysis of Decisions Under Risk," *Econometrica* 47(1979): 287.
2. This discussion is adapted from Richard Thaler and Eric Johnson, "Gambling with the House Money and Trying to Break Even: The Effects of Prior Outcomes on Risky Choice," *Management Science* 36(1990): 643–660.
3. Daniel Kahneman and Amos Tversky, "Prospect Theory: An Analysis of Decisions Under Risk," *Econometrica* 47(1979): 263–291.
4. Joshua Coval and Tyler Shumway, "Do Behavioral Biases Affect Prices?," Harvard Business School working paper, September, 2002.
5. Tracey Longo, "Stupid Investor Tricks," *Financial Planning* (April 2000): 116.
6. Richard Thaler, "Toward a Positive Theory of Consumer Choice," *Journal of Economic Behavior and Organization* 1(1980): 39–60.
7. William Samuelson and Richard Zeckhauser, "Status Quo Bias in Decision Making," *Journal of Risk and Uncertainty* 1(1988): 7–59.
8. Daniel Kahneman, Jack Knetsch, and Richard Thaler, "Experimental Tests of the Endowment Effect and the Coase Theorem," *Journal of Political Economy* 98(1990): 1325–1348; Kahneman, Knetsch, and Thaler, "Anomalies: The Endowment Effect, Loss Aversion, and Status Quo Bias," *Journal of Economic Perspectives* 1(1991): 193–206.
9. George Lowenstein and Daniel Kahneman, "Explaining the Endowment Effect," Carnegie Mellon University working paper (1991).
10. William Samuelson and Richard Zeckhauser, "Status Quo Bias in Decision Making," *Journal of Risk and Uncertainty* 1(1988): 7–59.
11. D. Kahneman, B. Fredrickson, C. Schreiber, and D. Redelmeier, "When More Pain Is Preferred to Less: Adding a Better End," *Psychological Science* (1993): 401–405.

12. This theory of "remembered utility" is discussed in Daniel Kahneman, Peter Wakker, and Rakesh Sarin, "Back to Bentham? Explorations of Experienced Utility," *Quarterly Journal of Economics* 112(1997): 375–406.
13. Daniel Read and George Lowenstein, "Enduring Pain for Money: Decisions Based on the Perception and Memory of Pain," *Journal of Behavioral Decision Making* 12(1999): 1–17.
14. The description of cognitive dissonance comes from George Akerlof and William Dickens, "The Economic Consequences of Cognitive Dissonance," *American Economic Review* 72(1982): 307–319.
15. Robert Knox and James Inkster, "Postdecision Dissonance at Post Time," *Journal of Personality and Social Psychology* 8(1968): 319–323.
16. William Goetzmann and Nadav Peles, "Cognitive Dissonance and Mutual Fund Investors," *Journal of Financial Research* 20(1997): 145–158.
17. Don Moore, Terri Kurtzberg, Craig Fox, and Max Bazerman, "Positive Illusions and Forecasting Errors in Mutual Fund Investment Decisions," *Organizational Behavior and Human Decision Processes* 79(1999): 95–114.

CHAPTER 5

Mental Accounting

Businesses, governments, and even churches use accounting systems to track, separate, and categorize the flow of money. People, on the other hand, use a mental accounting system. Imagine that your brain uses a mental accounting system similar to a file cabinet. Each decision, action, and outcome is placed in a separate file folder in the file cabinet. The folder contains the costs and benefits associated with a particular decision. Once an outcome is assigned to a mental folder, it is difficult to view that outcome in any other way. The ramifications of mental accounting are that it influences your decisions in unexpected ways.

Consider the following example.[1]

> Mr. and Mrs. J have saved $15,000 toward their dream vacation home. They hope to buy the home in 5 years. The money earns 4 percent in a money market account. They just bought a new car for $11,000, which they financed with a 3-year car loan at 9 percent.

This is a common situation. People have money in savings that earns a low rate of return and yet they borrow money at a high interest rate, thus losing money. In this example, the vacation home savings in the money market account is earning a rate of 4 percent. Imagine how excited Mr. and Mrs. J would be if they found a safe investment earning 9 percent! But when the 9 percent opportunity came up, they probably didn't even consider it. That opportunity was to borrow the $11,000 from their own savings (instead of the bank) and pay themselves a 9 percent interest rate. If they had done this, the vacation home savings in the money market account would have been more than $1,000 higher at the end of the 3 years.

Money does not come with labels, so people put labels on it. We've designated dirty money, easy money, free money, and so on. Mr. and Mrs. J labeled their savings as "vacation home" in a mental account.

Although mixing the "new car" mental account with the "vacation home" account would have maximized their wealth, Mr. and Mrs. J could not bring themselves to do it.

MENTAL BUDGETING

People use financial budgets to keep track of and control their spending. The brain uses mental budgets to associate the benefits of consumption with the costs in each mental account. Consider the pain (or costs) associated with the purchase of goods and services to be similar to that of the pain of financial losses. Similarly, the joy (or benefits) of consuming the goods and services is like the joy of financial gains. Mental budgeting matches the emotional pain to the emotional joy.

MATCHING COSTS TO BENEFITS

People usually prefer a "pay-as-you-go" payment system because it provides a tight match between the benefits and costs of the purchase. However, things get more complicated when the pay-as-you-go system is not available.

Consider the following set of questions that investigate the timing of payments. Professors Drazen Prelec and George Loewenstein asked 91 visitors to the Phipps Conservatory in Pittsburgh the following questions.[2] The first question is this.

> Imagine that 6 months from now, you are planning to purchase a clothes washer and dryer for your new residence. The two machines together will cost $1,200. You have two options for financing the washer/dryer:
>
> A. Six monthly payments of $200 each during the 6 months before the washer and dryer arrive.
>
> B. Six monthly payments of $200 each during the 6 months beginning after the washer and dryer arrive.

Which option would you choose? Note that the total cost is the same in both options; only the timing of the costs is different. Of the 91 people interviewed, 84 percent responded that they preferred the postponed payment schedule B. This is consistent with the cost/benefit matching of mental budgeting. The benefits of the washer and dryer will be used for a period of years after their purchase. Paying the cost over a concurrent period matches the cost to the benefit. Note that option B is also consistent with traditional economic theories. That is, people should choose B because it is less expensive after considering the time value of money.

The next two examples are not consistent with traditional economic theories, and respondents did not select the wealth-maximizing option. Consider this example.

> Imagine that you are planning to take a 1-week vacation to the Caribbean 6 months from now. The vacation will cost $1,200. You have two options for financing the vacation:
>
> A. Six monthly payments of $200 each during the 6 months before the vacation.
>
> B. Six monthly payments of $200 each during the 6 months beginning after you return.

Notice that the payment stream options are the same as in the prior question—six payments before or six payments after the purchase. The difference is that the item being purchased has changed. The main difference is that the vacation is a purchase whose benefits will be consumed in a short time, whereas the benefits of the washer and dryer will be consumed over the course of years. Which option would you choose?

Sixty percent of the respondents selected option A, the prepaid vacation. In this case, the payment options do not match with the consumption of the goods. The benefits of vacations are consumed during the vacation, but this vacation must be paid for either before or afterward.

Traditional economic theories predict that people will prefer option B because it is cheaper after considering the time value of money. However, most people choose option A. Why? People believe that a prepaid vacation is more pleasurable than one that must be paid for later, because the pain of payment is over. If payment is to be made later, the benefits of the vacation are diminished by wondering how much the pleasure is going to cost. An important factor in the "prepay or finance it" decision is the amount of pleasure expected to be generated by the purchase. The thought of paying for an item over the time that the item is being used reduces the pleasure of using that item. But let's face it: Using a washer and dryer is not that much fun anyway, so we might as well finance it. The dream home example at the beginning of this chapter is another matter. The pleasure of the dream home should not be tainted with debt and the thoughts of future payments; therefore, Mr. and Mrs. J are prepaying (saving for) the house.

The third question to the visitors addressed income from overtime work to be performed: How would you like to get paid for working a few hours on the weekends during the next 6 months? Prepayment for work to be done in the future was not desirable.

Sixty-six of the respondents preferred to get paid after doing the work instead of before. Again, this is not consistent with traditional economic theories. The wealth-maximizing option is to get paid earlier, not later.

AVERSION TO DEBT

In the vacation and overtime questions, people are expressing an aversion to debt when the good or service is consumed quickly. People show a preference for matching the length of the payments to the length of time the good or service is used. For example, using debt to purchase homes, cars, TVs, and so forth is popular because these items are consumed over many years. Using debt and paying off the purchase over time results in a strong match associated with the consumption of those items.

On the other hand, people do not like to make payments on a debt for a purchase that has already been consumed. Financing the vacation is undesirable because it causes a long-term cost on a short-term benefit. This is also true for the third question. People do not want to get prepaid for work because it creates a long-term debt (working weekends for the next 6 months) for a short-term benefit (getting paid). People prefer to do the work first and then get paid.

SUNK-COST EFFECT

Traditional economic theories predict that people will consider the present and future costs and benefits when determining a course of action. Past costs should not be a factor. Contrary to these predictions, people routinely consider historic, nonrecoverable costs when making decisions about the future. This behavior is called the sunk-cost effect.[3] The sunk-cost effect is an escalation of commitment and has been defined as the "greater tendency to continue an endeavor once an investment in money, time, or effect has been made."[4]

Sunk costs have two important dimensions: size and timing.[5] Consider the following two scenarios.

> A family has tickets to a basketball game, which they have been anticipating for some time. The tickets are worth $40. On the day of the game, a big snowstorm hits their area. Although they can still go to the game, the snowstorm will cause a hassle that will reduce the pleasure of watching the game. Is the family more likely to go to the game if they purchased the tickets for $40 or if the tickets were given to them for free?

The common belief is that the family is more likely to go to the game if they purchased the tickets. Note that the $40 cost of the ticket does not factor into the hassle of the snowstorm or the pleasure derived from the game. Yet, people consider the sunk cost in their decision whether or not to go. A family that pays for the tickets opens a mental account. If they do not attend the game, the family is forced to close the mental account without the benefit of the purchase, resulting in a perceived loss. The family wishes to avoid the emotional pain of the loss; therefore, they are more likely to go to the game. Had the tickets been free, the account could be closed without a benefit or a cost.

This example illustrates that the size of the sunk cost is an important factor in decision making. In both cases the family had tickets, but it was the cost of the tickets ($40 versus $0) that mattered. The next example illustrates that the timing of the sunk cost is also an important component.

> A family has long anticipated going to the basketball game, which will take place next week. On the day of the game, a snowstorm occurs. Is the family more likely to go to the game if they purchased the $40 tickets 1 year ago or yesterday?

In both cases, the $40 purchase price is a sunk cost. However, does the timing of the sunk cost matter? Yes, the family is more likely to go to the game if they purchased the tickets yesterday than if they purchased the tickets last year. The pain of closing a mental account without a benefit decreases with time. In short, the negative impact of a sunk cost depreciates over time.

ECONOMIC IMPACT

The previous examples demonstrate that people are willing to incur monetary costs to facilitate their mental budgeting process. Remember that people tend to prepay for some purchases, and they prefer to get paid *after* doing the work. By accelerating payments and delaying income, they are not taking advantage of the time value of money principles. Traditional economic theories predict that people would prefer the opposite: delaying payment and accelerating income to maximize the present value of their wealth.

Mental accounting causes people to want to match the emotional costs and benefits of a purchase. Their determination frequently leads to expensive decisions. Consider the following example.[6] Fifty-six MBA students were asked to select a loan to finance the $7,000 cost of a home-remodeling project. The project involved redecorating (new carpet, wallpaper, paint, and so on) and would last 4 years, at which point they would have to redecorate again. Two borrowing options were given. One loan had a 3-year term and an interest rate of 12 percent. The other was a 15-year loan with an 11 percent interest rate. Both loans could be prepaid without penalty.

Note that the long-term loan has a lower interest rate. In addition, the 15-year loan can be converted into a 3-year loan (that has a lower interest rate) by merely accelerating the payments. That is, you could calculate the monthly payment needed to pay off the 15-year loan in only 3 years. Because the interest rate on the 15-year loan is lower than on the 3-year loan, the monthly payments would be lower. When asked, 74 percent of the MBA students preferred the 3-year loan. These students indicated a willingness to incur monetary costs (in the form of a higher interest rate) to make it easier to integrate related costs and benefits. The students were willing to pay a higher interest rate in order to guarantee that the loan will be paid in only 3 years. This is an example of the self-control problem discussed in Chapter 10.

MENTAL ACCOUNTING AND INVESTING

Decision makers tend to place each investment into a separate mental account. Each investment is treated separately, and interactions are overlooked. This mental process can adversely affect an investor's wealth in several ways. First, mental accounting exacerbates the disposition effect discussed in Chapter 3. Recall that investors avoid selling stocks with losses because they do not want to experience the emotional pain of regret. Selling the losing stock closes the mental account, triggering regret.

Consider the wealth-maximizing strategy of conducting a tax swap.[7] A tax swap is when an investor sells a stock with losses and purchases a similar stock. For example, suppose you own Northwest Airlines stock, which has experienced a price decline along with the entire airline industry. You could sell the Northwest stock and purchase United Airlines stock. This tax swap allows you to capture the capital loss of Northwest stock to reduce your taxes while staying invested and waiting for the airline industry rebound.

Why isn't the tax swap strategy used more often? Investors tend to consider the selling of the loser stock as a closing of that mental account and the buying of the similar stock as an opening of a new mental account. This causes two outcomes that affect investors. First, the interaction between these two accounts increases the investor's wealth. Second, the closing of the loser account causes regret. Investors tend to ignore the interaction between accounts; therefore, investors act to avoid regret instead of to maximize wealth.

Mental budgeting compounds the aversion to selling losers. Consider how people value the timing of payments and benefits. As time passes, the purchase of the stock becomes a sunk cost. The emotional pain of wasting some of the sunk cost on a loser diminishes over time.[8] It may be less emotionally distressing for the investor to sell the losing stock later as opposed to earlier.

When investors do decide to sell a loser, they have a tendency to bundle more than one sale on the same day. Investors integrate the sale of losers to aggregate the losses and limit the feeling of regret to one time period. In other words, people may combine the separate mental accounts in losing positions and close them out all at once in order to minimize their regret. Alternatively, investors like to separate the sale of winners over several days to prolong the more favorable feeling. Sonya Lim studied the selling behavior of 158,000 brokerage accounts from 1991 to 1996.[9] She found that investors are likely to sell more than one losing stock on the same day. On the other hand, if a winner stock is sold, selling another winner stock on the same day is less likely.

The narrow framing aspect of mental accounting might also explain why most people do not invest in the stock market,[10] even though stocks have a high mean return. The stock market risk has nearly zero correlation with a person's other economic risk, namely, labor income risk and housing price risk. Therefore, adding even a small amount of stock market risk provides diversification of one's overall economic risk. However, in isolation, which is how people tend to view things, the stock market appears much riskier than labor income risk and housing price risk. Last, mental accounting also affects investors' perceptions of portfolio risks. The tendency to overlook the interaction between investments causes investors to misperceive the risk of adding a security to an existing portfolio. The next chapter describes how mental accounting leads to the building of portfolios layer by layer. Each layer represents the investment choices that satisfy various mental accounts. This process allows investors to meet the goals of each mental account separately. It does not lead to the benefits of diversification shown by portfolio theory. That is, this process does not necessarily lead to lower risk. Therefore, investors end up not maximizing their return given the level of risk they take.

Questions

1. Why do people save money in advance for a vacation but tend to finance a consumer purchase and pay later? What are the factors involved?
2. Why do investors tend to sell losing positions together, on the same day, and separate the sale of winning positions over several days?
3. How does the use of a tax swap overcome some psychological biases?

End Notes

1. Richard Thaler, "Mental Accounting and Consumer Choice," *Marketing Science* 4(1985): 199–214.
2. Drazen Prelec and George Loewenstein, "The Red and the Black: Mental Accounting of Savings and Debt," *Marketing Science* 17(1998): 4–28.
3. Richard Thaler, "Toward a Positive Theory of Consumer Choice," *Journal of Economics Behavior and Organization* 1(March 1980): 39–60.
4. From Hal Arkes and Catherine Blumer, "The Psychology of Sunk Cost," *Organizational Behavior and Human Decision Processes* 35(February 1985): 124.
5. This discussion is adapted from John Gourville and Dilip Soman, "Payment Depreciation: The Behavioral Effects of Temporally Separating Payments from Consumption," *Journal of Consumer Research* 25(1998): 160–174.
6. Eric Hirst, Edward Joyce, and Michael Schadewald, "Mental Accounting and Outcome Contiguity in Consumer-Borrowing Decisions," *Organizational Behavior and Human Decision Processes* 58(1994): 136–152.
7. This discussion is adapted from Hersh Shefrin and Meir Statman, "The Disposition to Sell Winners Too Early and Ride Losers Too Long: Theory and Evidence," *Journal of Finance* 40(1984): 777–790.
8. John Gourville and Dilip Soman, "Payment Depreciation: The Behavioral Effects of Temporally Separating Payments from Consumption," *Journal of Consumer Research* 25(1998): 173.
9. Sonya Seongyeon Lim, "Do Investors Integrate Losses and Segregate Gains? Mental Accounting and Investor Trading Decisions," The Ohio State University working paper, July 24, 2003.
10. Nicholas Barberis, Ming Huang, and Richard Thaler, "Individual Preferences, Monetary Gambles, and the Equity Premium," University of Chicago working paper, September 2003.

CHAPTER 6

Forming Portfolios

The previous chapter detailed how mental accounting is used to track the costs and benefits associated with each decision. Mental accounting also affects how you view your investment portfolios.

MODERN PORTFOLIO THEORY

Fifty years ago, the Nobel prize–winning economist Harry Markowitz taught us to consider all our investments as one whole portfolio. According to Markowitz, an investor should consider owning the investments that combine to form a portfolio that offers the highest expected return for the level of risk desired. Combining investments into a portfolio requires the investor to think in terms of diversification. Investors like the idea of diversification. However, they implement diversification differently than Markowitz's portfolio theory suggests.

To implement portfolio theory, you must consider three important characteristics of each potential investment. The first two parameters are the expected return and the level of risk (as measured by standard deviation of returns) of the investments. Examining the risk and return makes sense to investors. The third important characteristic is the correlation between the returns of each investment. Correlation is how each investment interacts with the others. Mental accounting makes it difficult to implement this important characteristic.

MENTAL ACCOUNTING AND PORTFOLIOS

Investors typically place each investment into a separate mental account. One outcome of mental accounting is that you discount the interaction between mental accounts, which affects the construction of your portfolio. Consider the high volatility of the recent stock market. Stocks often experience large price gains and losses each day. Modern portfolio theory shows that different investments can be combined to reduce this volatility. By comparing how the price of different investments changes over time, a lower-risk portfolio can be constructed.

For example, stocks A and B in Figure 6.1 have approximately the same return and variation in stock price over time. Both stocks experience large price changes. However, notice that when stock A is advancing, stock B is often declining. Because stocks A and B frequently move in opposite directions, buying both stocks creates a portfolio with reduced risk. That is, the value of your portfolio varies less over time when you own stocks A and B than it would if you owned only one of those stocks.

However, creating a portfolio that reduces risk (in the modern portfolio theory sense) means considering the interaction between different investments. Unfortunately, investors often treat each investment as a different mental account and tend to ignore the interaction between those mental accounts. Therefore, the most useful tool in constructing portfolios and reducing risk, the correlation between investments, is difficult to utilize because of mental accounting.[1]

Instead, portfolios are built by making buy decisions on each investment individually. In general, investors tend to pick investments

FIGURE 6.1 Combining Stocks into a Portfolio

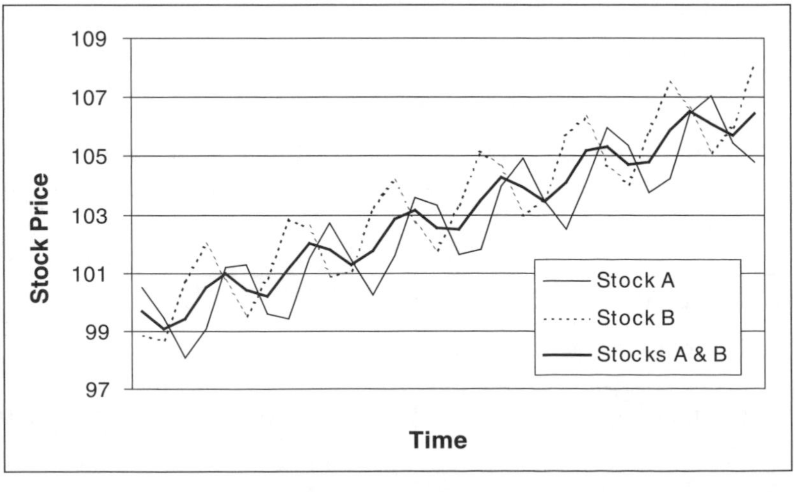

as if they were picking food at a buffet: "This looks interesting . . . I think I'll have some of that . . . maybe a little of this one . . . I've heard about that one. . . ." The decision to purchase a new security and open a new mental account does not include the investment's correlation with other investments because the mental accounts do not interact with each other.

PERCEPTIONS ON RISK

Viewing each investment as a separate mental account causes investors to misperceive risk. Investors evaluate each potential investment as if it were the only investment they will own. However, most investors already have a portfolio and are considering other investments to add to it. Therefore, the most important consideration for the evaluation is how the expected risk and return of the portfolio will change when a new investment is added. In other words, it is how the new investment interacts with the existing portfolio that matters. Unfortunately, people have trouble evaluating the interactions between mental accounts. Consider the following problem.

> You have a diversified portfolio of large domestic and international stocks with some fixed-income securities. You are examining the following investments: commodities, corporate bonds (high-grade), emerging markets stocks, European and East Asian stocks, high-yield bonds, real estate, Russell 2000 Growth Index, small capitalization stocks, and treasury bills. How does the addition of each investment change the risk of the existing portfolio?

I asked 45 undergraduate and 27 graduate students taking the investments course and 16 investment club participants to sort these nine investments by their level of risk contribution to the portfolio. Note that the experiment participants were not given return, risk, or correlation information. They had to make decisions based on their own knowledge and information. Figure 6.2 reports the results of the three groups.

Treasury bills and corporate bonds are viewed as adding the least risk, whereas real estate, commodities, and high-yield bonds add higher risk. Small capitalization stocks and foreign stocks add the most risk to the portfolio. Notice that all three groups provide a similar ranking of how each investment contributes risk to the existing portfolio. The last ranking in the figure was calculated using the investments' standard deviation of monthly returns during 1980

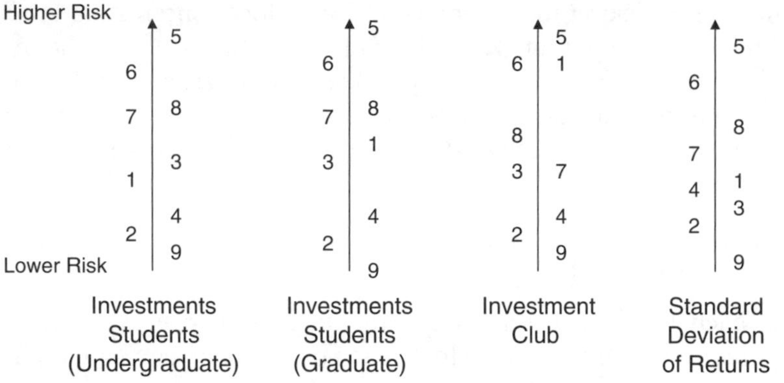

1. Commodities (gold, oil, etc.) 2. Corporate Bonds 3. High-Yield Corporate Bonds
4. Real Estate 5. Stocks from Emerging Market Countries 6. Stocks from Europe and East Asia
7. Small Capitalization Stocks 8. Small Capitalization Growth Stocks 9. Treasury Bill

FIGURE 6.2 Investor's View of Risk Contribution to Portfolio

to 1997.[2] Standard deviation is a good measure of an investment's risk. The rank order and magnitude of risk contribution of the three different groups is similar to the risk ranking using standard deviation as the measure.

However, standard deviation measures the riskiness of the investment, not how the risk of the portfolio would change if the investment were added. Remember the earlier example where stocks A and B had the same risk but combined to reduce risk in a portfolio? It is not the level of risk for each investment that is important; the important measure is how each investment interacts with the existing portfolio. Consider Figure 6.3A.

Panel A of the figure plots the standard deviation of monthly stock returns for each investment versus the investment's contribution of risk to the existing portfolio, as measured by beta. A beta of greater than 1 indicates that the investment would increase the risk of the portfolio. A beta smaller than 1 indicates that adding the security would reduce the risk of the portfolio.

Notice that the last risk ranking in Figure 6.2 is simply the *y*-axis of Figure 6.3A. Because of mental accounting, investors view the risk of adding an investment to their portfolio as the individual risk (standard deviation) of the investment. However, the real contribution to portfolio risk of the investment is measured on the *x*-axis.

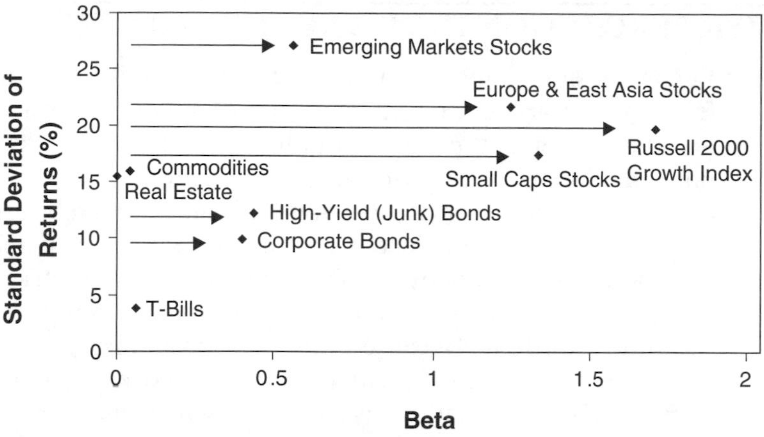

FIGURE 6.3A Investment Risk and Risk Contribution to Portfolio

Figure 6.3B shows just the *x*-axis—the interaction between the investment and the existing portfolio.

Panel B shows that if you want to reduce the risk of your portfolio, you should add real estate and commodities. Does this come as a surprise? Small capitalization stocks and Russell 2000 Growth Index–type stocks increase the risk of the portfolio. Viewed by themselves, emerging markets stocks are the most risky investments in the example. However, they would interact with the existing portfolio such that they would reduce the risk of the portfolio, if they were added.

FIGURE 6.3B Change in Portfolio Risk After Adding the Investment

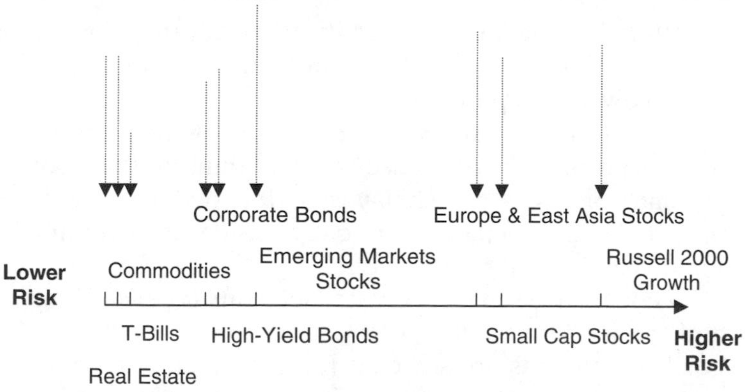

RISK PERCEPTION IN THE REAL WORLD

Public pension systems demonstrate how the misperception of risk from mental accounting affects portfolios. Public pension systems are the retirement plans of public employees such as teachers, police, and state and city workers. The state or local government sets aside money each year to be invested and ultimately used as the employees' retirement income. Professional money managers are hired to invest the money, but the government may restrict the managers from investing in specific securities in an attempt to limit the risk of the portfolio. Because of mental accounting, the government officials tend to use each security's individual risk (as in Figure 6.3B) instead of the interaction risk effect (as in Figure 6.3B) to make these decisions.

The Government Finance Officers Association surveyed public pension plans in 1999. These plans were asked about the investment restrictions under which they operate. A total of 211 retirement plans gave responses.[3] Remember that Figure 6.3B showed that real estate, corporate bonds, and even foreign stocks can reduce the risk of a typical portfolio. However, 14 plans responded that they could not invest in real estate. A total of 8 plans could not invest in corporate bonds, and 19 plans could not invest in foreign securities. Many more plans have other limitations, such as a maximum investment in real estate, corporate bonds, and foreign securities of no more than 5 percent of the portfolio. Interestingly, 3 plans could not invest in U.S. stocks at all. Those government policy makers need to take a finance course!

BUILDING BEHAVIORAL PORTFOLIOS

Investors like the idea of diversification, but they don't build portfolios in a manner suggested by portfolio theory. How, then, do investors build a diversified portfolio?

Hersh Shefrin and Meir Statman show how the psychological tendencies of investors cause them to think of their portfolios as a pyramid of assets.[4] Each layer in the pyramid represents assets intended to meet a particular goal. Consider the pyramid depicted in Figure 6.4.

People have separate mental accounts for each investment goal, and the investor is willing to take different levels of risk for each goal. Investments are selected for each mental account by finding assets that match the expected risk and return of the mental account.

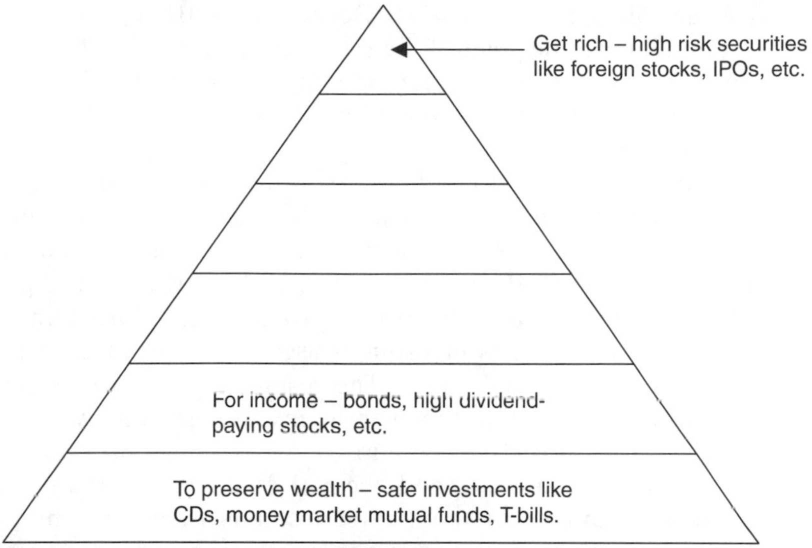

FIGURE 6.4 Pyramid Depicting Behavioral Portfolio

First, investors have a goal of safety. Therefore, they allocate enough assets in the safest layer (the bottom of the pyramid), as required by their mental accounts. Then mental accounts with higher levels of expected return and risk tolerance could allocate assets to appropriate investments in another layer. For example, retired investors need investment income. The income goal is met in a layer of the pyramid with assets invested in bonds and stocks that pay high dividends. After the income goal is met, the retiree's next goal might be to keep up with inflation. This investor would then have a set of assets in a layer that invests for growth.

Each mental account has an amount of money designated for that particular goal. It is the number of mental accounts requiring safety that determines the amount of money placed in safe investments. In contrast, some mental accounts designate the "get-rich" assets. In sum, the total asset allocation of an investor's portfolio is determined by how much money is designated for each asset class by the mental accounts. Investors without many safety-oriented goals will place a greater amount of money in high-risk securities. Investors who have stronger safety or income goals will have more securities in those layers of the pyramid.

Consider the average investor. The average investor has assets in a 401(k) pension plan that seem well diversified to the employee (but see the next two sections). Because the 401(k) plan matches the retirement income goals of the person, the next level of the pyramid might be to achieve a higher standard of living in retirement or to save for a child's college education. Mutual fund investments fit this goal nicely.

Higher up the pyramid, a person may want to become rich. A discount brokerage account can be used to try to meet this goal. The median number of stocks owned in a brokerage account is only three,[5] and the median investor trades about three times per year. This low level of diversification is probably not a problem because the investor likely has investment assets in other places (like pension plans and mutual funds). The result of these various goals and mental accounts is that the average investor ends up with a variety of mini-portfolios. The makeup of the overall portfolio is determined, formed, and changed because of the distribution of investment goals and associated mental accounts. Investors tend to overlook the interaction among mental accounts and among investment assets. As a result, investor diversification comes from investment goal diversification rather than from a purposeful asset diversification, as described in Markowitz's portfolio theory.

Ultimately, this means that most investors do not have efficient portfolios. As a consequence, investors are taking too much risk for the level of expected return they are getting. Stated another way, investors could obtain higher returns for the level of risk they are taking.

NAÏVE DIVERSIFICATION

Although investors should consider their entire portfolio when making investment decisions, they usually make decisions only within the narrow context of the situation. For example, consider investing for your retirement. Some of your assets will be in retirement plans, such as IRAs and 401(k) plans, and other assets will not be. Suppose the most efficient portfolio for you includes 50 percent stocks and 50 percent bonds. You probably will put half of your retirement plan money in stocks and half in bonds. You will do the same with the assets outside the retirements plans. However, this is not the best allocation. The reason is that you have to pay taxes on income from assets outside the retirement plans, such as from your bonds.

The better choice would be to invest the money within the retirement plans in bonds and buy the stocks with the assets outside the retirement plans. The overall portfolio would still be a mix of 50 percent stocks and 50 percent bonds, but you would owe less in taxes every year. However, this allocation is hard for investors because the conservative allocation of bonds in the retirement plans does not match their investing goals as indicated by the retirement mental account.

RETIREMENT PLANS

The 401(k) retirement plan is a good example of investor mental accounting and naïve diversification. Employers offer different investment choices within the 401(k) plans. For example, one plan may have one bond fund and three stock funds to choose from, and another plan may have one bond fund and one stock fund. Which investments do employees choose?

Employees have a tendency to diversify their 401(k) investments by using a 1/*n* rule. The old adage says that we should "never put all our eggs in one basket." But the adage doesn't give us any direction on how to distribute our eggs. Should we divide them evenly between baskets? If three 401(k) choices are available, should we allocate one-third to each of the three choices?

Interestingly, this occurs no matter what the choices are. For example, the plan offered to TWA pilots has five stocks funds and one bond fund. If all pilots use the 1/*n* rule, then we should expect 83 percent (5/6) of the average portfolio to be invested in stocks. Indeed, the TWA pilots invest an average of 75 percent in stocks, which is much higher than the 57 percent national average. Alternatively, the University of California (UC) employees are offered one stock fund and four bond funds. The average stock holdings for UC employees amount to only 34 percent. Indeed, the number and type of investment offerings seem to play an important role in the asset allocation of employees. At least some employees appear to use the naïve diversification rule of 1/*n*.[6]

Another example is the mental accounting of company stock in the 401(k) plan. Employees appear to treat the stock of the company they work for as different from other stocks. A 1995 survey by John Hancock Financial Services found that a majority of employees believe their own company stock is safer than a diversified portfolio.

Company stock is frequently one of the 401(k) choices for employees. In a study of 170 different corporate 401(k) plans, Shlomo Benartzi and Richard Thaler found that 103 plans include company stock as an option. Of the 67 plans that did not include company stock, employees allocated 49.2 percent of their assets to stocks. This nearly 50–50 split is common. However, employees who have the company stock as an option have an average of 42 percent of their assets in the company stock. If they also want a 50–50 split between stocks and bonds, then they should invest most of the rest of their assets in bonds. However, they do not do this. Instead, they split the rest of their assets 50–50 between stocks and bonds. In this way, employees in plans with company stock end up having an average of 71 percent of their portfolio in stocks. These investors appear to put their company stock into its own mental account that is not associated with other stocks.

The tools of traditional finance, like modern portfolio theory, can help investors establish efficient portfolios to maximize their wealth with acceptable levels of risk. However, mental accounting makes it difficult to implement these tools. Instead, investors use mental accounting to match different investing goals to different asset allocations. This often leads to investors diversifying their portfolio by investing in all of the alternatives before them, regardless of the type of alternatives.

Even investors who overcome their tendency toward mental accounting and implement modern portfolio efficiency in their portfolios often find themselves second-guessing. The concept of integrating asset classes that exhibit a low correlation means that one or more asset classes held probably will be performing poorly at any given time. Even investors who believe in the diversification argument find themselves pointing to the under-performing asset class in their portfolios and wanting out of it.

Questions

1. How does mental accounting make the concepts of correlation difficult for investors to implement?
2. Consider a family of 40-something parents and teenage children. If the family forms its portfolio through a behavioral process, what might it look like? Compare it with what a portfolio would look like if formed on modern portfolio theory principles.
3. How does the number of investment choices tend to affect the allocation in an employee's 401(k) plan?

End Notes

1. Roger G. Clarke, Scott Krase, and Meir Statman, "Tracking Errors, Regret, and Tactical Asset Allocation," *Journal of Portfolio Management* 20(1994): 16–24.
2. Data for these figures come from Table 3.7 (page 93) of Frank K. Reilly and Keith C. Brown, *Investment Analysis and Portfolio Management,* Dryden Press, Harcourt College Publishers, 2000.

3. These results are calculated using the Pendat 2000 Database, which can be obtained from the Government Finance Officers Association.
4. Hersh Shefrin and Meir Statman, "Behavioral Portfolio Theory," *Journal of Financial and Quantitative Analysis* 35(2000): 127–151; Meir Statman, "Foreign Stocks in Behavioral Portfolios," *Financial Analysts Journal* (March/April 1999): 12–16.
5. Ravi Dhar and Ning Zhu, "Up Close and Personal: An Individual Level Analysis of the Disposition Effect," Yale ICF working paper # 02-20, August 2002.
6. This example and others can be found in Shlomo Benartzi and Richard H. Thaler, "Naïve Diversification Strategies in Defined Contribution Savings Plans," *American Economic Review* 91(2001): 79–98.

CHAPTER 7

Representativeness and Familiarity

Psychological research has shown that the brain uses shortcuts to reduce the complexity of analyzing information. These shortcuts allow the brain to generate an estimate of the answer before fully digesting all the available information. Two examples of shortcuts are known as representativeness and familiarity. Using these shortcuts allows the brain to organize and quickly process large amounts of information. However, these shortcuts also make it hard for investors to analyze new information correctly and can lead to inaccurate conclusions.

REPRESENTATIVENESS

The brain makes the assumption that things that share similar qualities are quite alike. Representativeness is judgment based on stereotypes. Consider the following question.

> Mary is quiet, studious, and concerned with social issues. While an undergraduate at Berkeley, she majored in English literature and environmental studies. Given this information, indicate which of the following three cases is most probable.
>
> A. Mary is a librarian.
> B. Mary is a librarian and a member of the Sierra Club.
> C. Mary works in the banking industry.

I have asked this question to undergraduate investment students, MBA graduate students, and financial advisors. In all three cases, more than half the subjects choose answer B—Mary is a librarian and a member of the Sierra Club. People select this answer because being a librarian and a member of the Sierra Club is representative of the type of career a studious person concerned with social issues might pick.

However, the question asked which case is more probable, not which case would make Mary the happiest.

Answer A—Mary is a librarian—is a superior answer to B. Being a librarian and a Sierra Club member is also being a librarian. That is, answer B is a subset of answer A. Because answer A includes answer B, it is more probable that case A is true. A quarter to a third of the subjects asked usually understand this and choose answer A over answer B.

However, the best answer is case C—Mary works in the banking industry. Many more people are employed by banks than by libraries. If fact, so many more jobs exist in banking that it is far more probable that someone works in the banking industry than as a librarian. Because working in the banking industry is not "representative" of the shortcut our brain makes to describe Mary, few people pick answer C.

REPRESENTATIVENESS AND INVESTING

People also make representativeness errors in financial markets. For example, investors confuse a good company with a good investment. Good companies are represented by firms that generate strong earnings, have high sales growth, and have quality management. Good investments are stocks that increase in price more than other stocks. Are the stocks of good companies good investments? The answer might be no.[1]

Classifying good stocks as firms with a history of consistent earnings growth ignores the fact that few companies can sustain the high levels of growth achieved in the past. The popularity of these firms drives prices higher. However, over time it becomes apparent that investors have been too optimistic in predicting future growth, and the stock price falls. This is known as overreaction.[2]

Three financial economists examined this issue. Josef Lakonishok, Andrei Shleifer, and Robert Vishny (henceforth L, S, & V) studied the performance of stocks investors typically consider to be growth stocks. These researchers label growth stocks as "glamour" stocks. Stocks of firms that investors typically consider to be bad firms with minimal growth prospects are labeled "value" stocks. Investors consider growth firms to be firms with growing business operations. L, S, & V calculated the average growth rate in sales for all firms over the past 5 years. The 10 percent of firms with the highest average growth rates were glamour firms, whereas the firms with the lowest sales growth were value firms. Glamour or value—which stocks will be better investments over the next year? The next 5 years?

Using data for all stocks on the New York Stock Exchange and American Stock Exchange over the period 1963 to 1990, L, S, & V reported the results in Figure 7.1.[3] If you bought the glamour stocks, you earned an 11.4 percent return the following year. This compares with a return of 18.7 percent for the value stocks. The average total return over a 5-year period is 81.8 percent for the glamour stocks and 143.4 percent for the value stocks.

Another popular measure of glamour/value stocks is the profit/earnings (P/E) ratio. Companies with high P/E ratios are more glamorous than firms with low P/E ratios. The figure also demonstrates that value stocks outperform glamour stocks using the P/E ratio measure.

Good companies do not always make good investments. Investors often erroneously believe that the past operating performance of the firm is representative of the future performance, and they ignore information that does not fit this notion. Good companies do not perform well forever, just as bad companies do not perform poorly forever.

FIGURE 7.1 One-Year and Five-Year Returns for Glamour and Value Stocks

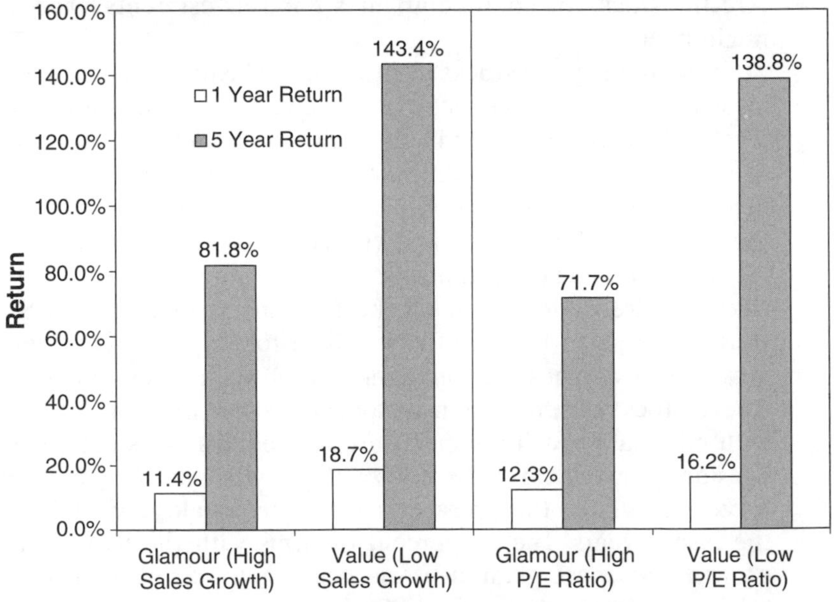

Source: Josef Lakonishok, Andrei Shleifer, and Robert Vishny, "Contrarian Investment, Extrapolation, and Risk," *Journal of Finance* 48(1994): 1541–1578.

Investors also make this error of extrapolating when examining past stock returns. For example, a stock that has performed badly for the past 3 to 5 years is considered a loser. On the other hand, stocks that have done great for the past 3 to 5 years are considered winners. Investors assume this past return is representative of what they can expect in the future. Investors like to chase the winners and buy firms that have trended upward in price.[4] However, the losers tend to outperform the winners over the next 3 years by 30 percent.[5]

Mutual fund investors also make this same extrapolating error. The mutual funds listed in magazines and newspapers with the highest recent performance receive a flood of new investors. These investors are chasing the winners.

Indeed, this type of investing is so popular that it has its own name: momentum investing. Momentum investors look for stocks and mutual funds that have performed well over the past week, month, or quarter. Momentum traders look for good performers over the past few hours or even minutes. The media exacerbate the bias. For example, every day, the *Wall Street Journal* reports yesterday's biggest percentage gainers, and throughout the day, CNBC announces which stocks have the highest price change for the day.

Even finance professors are influenced by the representativeness bias. Ivo Welch has implemented several surveys of financial economics professors.[6] The first series of surveys was implemented in 1997 through 1998, and an additional survey was conducted in 1999. These surveys elicited 226 responses. Note that these surveys were completed during a strong bull market. One question asked about the expected annual equity risk premium over the next 30 years. The mean response was 7.2 percent. In a separate question about stock market return mean reversion versus the random walk, the professors tended to lean toward the belief that the stock market mean reverts. Welch again surveyed the profession in 2001, when the market environment was quite different. The S&P 500 Index had declined by approximately 25 percent from its peak. Given the earlier expression that stock returns might exhibit mean reversion, we might expect respondents to express a higher equity premium estimate after a market decline. However, the mean annual 30-year equity risk premium was only 5.5 percent. Note that this is considerably lower than estimates provided only 3 years earlier. Although their updated estimates were about 2 percent lower, they reiterated their belief that stock returns are mean reverting. Yet, their estimates are not consistent with that belief. The responses are consistent with the notion that the most recent past is representative of what will happen in the future.

In short, investors interpret the past business operations of a firm and the past performance of stock as representative of future expectations. Unfortunately, firms tend to revert to the mean over the long term. That is, fast-growing firms find that competition increases and slows their rate of growth. Disappointed investors, in turn, find that the stock **does not perform as expected.**

FAMILIARITY

People prefer things that are familiar to them. Fans root for the local sports teams, and employees like to own their company's stock. This is because the sports teams and the company are familiar to them.

When people are faced with two risky choices and they know more about one than the other, they will pick the more familiar option. Given two different gambles in which the odds of winning are the same but they have more experience with one over the other, people pick the better-known gamble. In fact, they will sometimes pick the more familiar gamble even if the odds of winning are lower.[7]

FAMILIARITY BREEDS INVESTMENT

Tens of thousands of potential stock and bond investments exist in the United States with that many choices overseas, as well. So how do investors choose? Do we analyze the expected return and risk of each investment? No, investors trade in the securities with which they are familiar.[8] There is comfort in having your money invested in a business that is visible to you.

As an example, consider the breakup of AT&T. In 1984, the government broke up AT&T's local phone service monopoly into seven regional phone companies known as the "Baby Bells." Twelve years after the breakup, Gur Huberman investigated the ownership of these Baby Bells. He found that investors are more likely to own shares in their local phone company than the phone company of another region; that is, they are more comfortable investing in the more familiar firm. This preference for investing close to home also applies to investment managers.[9]

The inclination to invest in the familiar causes people to invest far more money within their own country than traditional ideas of diversification would suggest. Investors have a "home bias" because companies from their own country are more familiar to them than foreign companies.

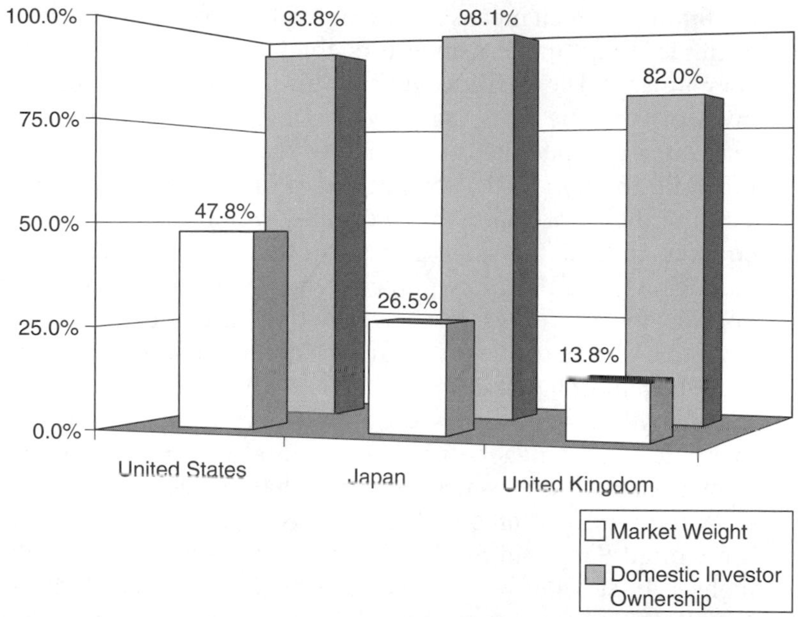

FIGURE 7.2 Market Weight of Country's Stock Market Compared to Total World (foreground) and the Percentage of the Country's Stock Market Owned by Domestic Investors (background)

Figure 7.2 illustrates the home bias.[10] The stock market in the United States represents 47.8 percent of the value of all stocks worldwide. The stock markets in Japan and the United Kingdom represent 26.5 percent and 13.8 percent of the worldwide stock market, respectively. Therefore, to fully diversify a stock portfolio, investors should allocate 47.8 percent of their portfolio to U.S. stocks, 26.5 percent to Japanese stocks, and 13.8 percent to U.K. stocks. In fact, traditional portfolio theory suggests that all investors should have this allocation.

Do real investors use this allocation? No. The stock portfolios of U.S. investors are 93 percent invested in U.S. stocks, not the 47.8 percent predicted by portfolio theory. Japanese investors are 98 percent invested in Japanese stocks, and U.K. investors have 82 percent of their stock portfolio in U.K. stocks. As these numbers show, investors purchase the stocks of companies that are familiar to them, and people generally are less familiar with foreign firms.

When people do invest some of their money in foreign firms, what types of foreign firms do they buy? They buy foreign firms that are familiar, which means large firms with recognizable products. For example, non-Japanese investors tend to own the large Japanese companies.[11] The smaller Japanese firms that attract non-Japanese investors are the ones that have high levels of exports. Chapter 6 illustrated that people do not think of their portfolios from a modern portfolio theory (MPT) perspective. If investors did use MPT when forming their portfolios, they probably would own far more foreign equities. Indeed, the small allocation that investors place in foreign equities implies that they perceive the riskiness of foreign assets to be two to five times larger than they historically have been.[12] Investors also perceive the return of familiar assets to be higher than those of unfamiliar assets.

Merrill Lynch surveys fund managers from around the world every month. Managers from Continental Europe predict that their domestic stock returns will be higher than those of the United Kingdom, the United States, and Japan.[13] At the same time, managers in the United Kingdom predict that their domestic returns will be the highest. In short, investors are more bullish on their domestic market relative to foreign markets. The familiarity bias causes investors to be too confident in stocks that are familiar, judging them too optimistically on expected return and risk. Likewise, the stocks that are unfamiliar are judged too pessimistically on risk and return.

People in the United States pick familiar foreign firms and bias their portfolios toward U.S. companies. Investors also tilt their portfolios toward local firms. For example, Coca-Cola's headquarters is located in Atlanta, Georgia. Investors living in Georgia own 16 percent of Coke,[14] and the majority of these investors live in Atlanta. Coke sells its products worldwide, but the people most familiar with the company own a large percentage of it.

Professional money managers also invest in the familiar. Even though U.S. professional investors have access to vast information sources and analysis tools, they tilt their portfolios toward local firms. This is especially true for local small firms and riskier firms. On average, the firms that a professional money manager buys are headquartered 100 miles closer to the manager's office than the typical U.S. company.[15]

FAMILIARITY BREEDS INVESTMENT PROBLEMS

What company are you most familiar with? People are generally most familiar with the company they work for. This familiarity causes employees to invest their pension money in the company stock. For example, a company 401(k) pension plan allows employees to invest money in options like a diversified stock fund, a bond fund, and money market instruments. One common option is the company's stock.

Traditional portfolio theory suggests that employees should diversify their retirement assets by selecting diversified stock, bond, and money market funds as needed according to their risk tolerance. Selecting the stock of one company is not practicing diversification. Considering that people already have their labor capital tied up in the company, to fully diversify, they should avoid investing their financial capital, too.

If your job and your retirement assets depend on one company, you could be in for a shock. Consider the plight of the employees of companies like Enron and Global Crossing. Measuring from the stock price peak values, the proportion of Enron employee 401(k) assets invested in Enron stock was 60 percent. The proportion of company stock in the Global Crossing 401(k) plan reached 53 percent. After declaring bankruptcy, the thousands of Enron employees saw 401(k) losses of $1.3 billion. After the Enron and Global Crossing bankruptcies, the media wrote about employees who had their entire retirement fund invested in the company stock, which became worthless. Many of these people also lost their jobs.

Is it common for employees to invest their retirement money in their company's stock? Yes. In a survey of 246 of America's largest companies, 42 percent of the total 401(k) plan assets were invested in the company stock.[16] Employees themselves make this decision. They like investing in the company stock because it is familiar. This is dangerous!

When you are familiar with something, you have a distorted perception of it. Fans of a sports team think their team has a higher chance of winning than non-fans of the team. Likewise, investors look favorably on investments they are familiar with, believing they will deliver higher returns and have less risk than unfamiliar investments. For example, Americans believe the U.S. stock market will perform better than the German stock market; meanwhile, Germans believe their stock market will perform better.[17] Similarly, employees believe the stock of their employer is a safer investment than a diversified stock portfolio.[18]

Over-concentrating a portfolio in only one stock is risky. However, employees do not want to believe that about the stock of their company. The Morningstar.com Web site asked investors this question: Which is more likely to lose half of its value, your firm or the overall stock market? It is far more likely that any single company would experience such a large price move than a diversified portfolio, especially the overall market. However, more than 1,000 investors responded to the question, and only 16.4 percent of the respondents believed their company was riskier than the overall stock market.[19] Of those investors without a college education, only 6.5 percent believed their company was riskier than the stock market. No one company is safer than a fully diversified portfolio like the overall stock market, so the familiarity bias clearly influences one's perception of risk.

The brain often uses the familiarity shortcut to evaluate investments. This can cause people to invest too much money in the stocks that are most familiar to them, like their employer's stock. Ultimately, this leads to a lack of diversification. In summary, investors allocate too much of their wealth to their employer, local companies, and domestic stocks.

COMBINING FAMILIARITY AND REPRESENTATIVENESS BIASES

Employees often compound the familiarity bias by combining it with the representativeness bias. Consider the ownership of company stock in employees' 401(k) plans. Employees tend to buy more of their company's stock after its price increases.[20] Employees who work for a company whose stock price increase ranked among the top 20 percent of all firms in the past 5 years allocated 31 percent of their contributions to the company stock. This compares to an allocation of only 13 percent to company stock in firms whose performance was in the worst 20 percent. The actual 401(k) asset allocation behavior of employees suggests that they use the past price trend (the representativeness bias) as a determinant for investing in the company stock (the familiarity bias). However, this is not a case of employees, as insiders, having good information about their firm. Firms with high employee pension plan ownership did not perform any better, on average, than those with low employee pension plan ownership.

Questions

1. A statement found in every mutual fund prospectus is "Past performance is not indicative of future performance." Yet, investors tend to use past performance as an important factor in making investment decisions. Why?
2. Why do investors in one country believe the return will be better and the risk is lower in their own country's stock market than in other countries' markets?
3. How do the familiarity bias and the representativeness bias combine to influence the 401(k) pension plan choices of employees?

End Notes

1. See discussions in the following sources: Hersh Shefrin, *Beyond Green and Fear: Understanding Behavioral Finance and the Psychology of Investing,* Boston: Harvard Business School Press, 2000; Hersh Shefrin and Meir Statman, "Making Sense of Beta, Size, and Book-to-Market," *Journal of Portfolio Management* (1995): 26–34; Michael Solt and Meir Statman, "Good Companies, Bad Stocks," *Journal of Portfolio Management* (1989): 39–44.
2. See the empirical evidence in Werner De Bondt and Richard Thaler, "Does the Stock Market Overreact?" *Journal of Finance* 40(1985): 793–808; and the theoretical model of Nicholas Barberis, Andrei Shleifer, and Robert Vishny, "A Model of Investor Sentiment," *Journal of Financial Economics* 49(1998): 307–343.
3. See panels C and D of Table 1 in Josef Lakonishok, Andrei Shleifer, and Robert Vishny, "Contrarian Investment, Extrapolation, and Risk," *Journal of Finance* 48(1994): 1541–1578.
4. Werner De Bondt, "Betting on Trends: Intuitive Forecasts of Financial Risk and Return," *International Journal of Forecasting* 9(1993): 355–371.
5. Werner De Bondt and Richard Thaler, "Does the Stock Market Overreact?" *Journal of Finance* 40(1985): 793–808.
6. Ivo Welch, "Views of Financial Economists on the Equity Premium and on Professional Controversies," *Journal of Business* 73(2000): 501–537; Ivo Welch, "The Equity Premium Consensus Forecast Revisited," Cowles Foundation discussion paper no. 1325, September 2001.
7. Chip Heath and Amos Tversky, "Preferences and Beliefs: Ambiguity and Competence in Choice Under Uncertainty," *Journal of Risk and Uncertainty* 4(1991): 5–28.
8. Much of this discussion is adapted from Gur Huberman, "Familiarity Breeds Investment," *Review of Financial Studies* 14(2001): 659–680.
9. Joshua Coval and Tobias Moskowitz, "Home Bias at Home: Local Equity Preference in Domestic Portfolios," *Journal of Finance* 54(1999): 2045–2073.
10. The data for the figure come from Table 1 of Kenneth French and James Poterba, "Investor Diversification and International Equity Markets," *American Economic Review* 81(1991): 222–226.
11. Jun-Koo Kang and Rene Stulz, "Why Is There a Home Bias? An Analysis of Foreign Portfolio Equity Ownership in Japan," *Journal of Financial Economics* 46(1997): 3–28.
12. Kai Li, "Confidence in the Familiar: An International Perspective," Forthcoming, *Journal of Financial and Quantitative Analysis.*
13. Norman Strong and Xinzhong Xu, "Understanding the Equity Home Bias: Evidence from Survey Data," *Review of Economics and Statistics* 85(2003): 307–312.
14. N. Deogun, "The Legacy: Roberto Goizueta Led Coca-Cola Stock Surge, and Its Home Prospers," *Wall Street Journal,* Oct. 20, 1997, page A1.
15. Joshua Coval and Tobias Moskowitz, "Home Bias at Home: Local Equity Preference in Domestic Portfolios," *Journal of Finance* 54(1999): 2045–2073.
16. E. Schultz, "Color Tile Offers Sad Lessons for Investors in 401(k) Plans," *Wall Street Journal,* June 5, 1996, page C1; E. Schultz, "Workers Put Too Much in Their Employer's Stock," *Wall Street Journal,* Sept. 13, 1996, page C1.

17. M. Kilka and M. Weber, "Home Bias in International Stock Return Expectations," *Journal of Psychology and Financial Markets* 1(2000): 176–193.
18. K. Driscoll, J. Malcolm, M. Sirull, and P. Slotter, "1995 Gallup Survey of Defined Contribution Plan Participants," John Hancock Financial Services, Nov. 1995.
19. Shlomo Benartzi, "Excessive Extrapolation and the Allocation of 401(k) Accounts to Company Stock," *The Journal of Finance* 56(2001): 1747–1764.
20. Ibid.

CHAPTER 8

Social Interaction and Investing

People learn through interacting with other people. We watch the behavior of others to interpret their beliefs, but mostly we enjoy the social interaction of conversation; that is, we like to talk. We talk about subjects that excite us, topics that interest us, and even topics that worry us. Talking is an important way to obtain information and detect emotional reactions, which help form our opinions.

Our culture has experienced at least one tremendous shift in what we talk about over the last couple of decades. I refer to investment talk. The social norms of investment chat have changed dramatically. It was not so long ago that people avoided talking about investing. Asking someone about his or her mutual funds or talking about your stocks just wasn't done in a social setting.

Now, investment talk is heard everywhere. the financial channel, CNBC, was only launched in April 1989, yet when you go out to lunch, you'll often find it is being shown on the television. Other financially oriented cable channels, such as CNN FN (December 1995) and Bloomberg TV, followed CNBC's launch. Now dozens of regional and national radio shows dedicated to investing are being aired. This change in our social norms has had a dramatic impact on our investment behavior. As more people talk about investing, others become interested, too.

This shift in our society has had a dramatic impact on personal investment levels. Consider that in 1989, only 31.6 percent of American households owned stock. This ownership consisted of investments in the stock market, mutual funds, or retirement plans such as 401(k) plans. By 1995, the participation rate in the stock market had risen to 40.4 percent. In 1998, 48.9 percent of households were invested in stocks in one form or another.[1] In the span of less than 10 years, American households experienced a 50 percent increase in stock ownership. The more we talk about investing, the more we do it.

TALKING THE TALK

Conversation allows for the rapid exchange of information, opinions, and emotions. This is important for the stock market and investing. Stock brokers converse with clients and other brokers. Analysts communicate with executives and managers, and they form local groups and associations to interact with each other. Institutional investors form groups for sharing information. Individual investors talk to family members, neighbors, colleagues, and friends about investing.

For example, a survey of 156 high-income investors showed that more than half the time that an investor becomes interested in a stock, it is because another person mentioned it.[2] In addition, the survey found that since buying the stock, the new investor had spoken to an average of 20 other people about the company.

Because information is obtained and decisions are formed through talking with others, social people are more likely to learn about investing than less social people. As a consequence, highly social people are more likely to invest in the stock market or to participate in their 401(k) plan. A group of researchers studied the relationship between socially active households and participation in the stock market.[3] A social household is characterized as one in which its members interact with neighbors or attend church. The researchers used responses from a survey of 7,500 households in the Health and Retirement Study of Households. They found that social households are more likely to invest in the stock market than nonsocial households, and social households that live in areas with high stock market participation are even more likely to invest in the stock market if they are socially active. Therefore, the social interaction influence is magnified when the person is in the right environment—one that has investors in it.

SOCIAL ENVIRONMENT

You can be judged by the friends you keep, according to one old saying. But does your social group affect your wealth? The answer appears to be yes. People in a peer group tend to develop the same tastes and interests as well as the desire to live a similar lifestyle. Peer groups develop social norms according to the preferred beliefs of the group. Beliefs about investing are also a part of these social norms. If investing is not valued by the peer group, the conversation will rarely (if ever) turn toward investment topics.

Another peer group might discuss stocks frequently. The social environment impacts one's investment decisions.

One common example is participation in a 401(k) retirement plan (or other contribution plan). Due to the tax advantages, contributing to a retirement plan is a wise decision. If the employer also contributes in some matching way, that is even better. Yet many (even most) people do not participate. Education and wage levels are a determinant of participation in the 401(k) plan; however, the social norms of employees also impact the participation decision.

To illustrate how dramatic the peer effect can be, consider the participation rate of 436 university librarians.[4] These librarians work in 11 different buildings throughout campus. Librarians are highly educated people. In addition, they are specifically trained in how to find information. Surely, librarians should make the wise choice and contribute to their retirement plan. The participation rates for the librarians in each of the 11 buildings are shown in Figure 8.1. Note the large difference in participation rates. In one building, 73 percent of the librarians participate, but in a different building only 14 percent participate.

FIGURE 8.1 Pension Plan Participation Rates for 436 Librarians in 11 Locations

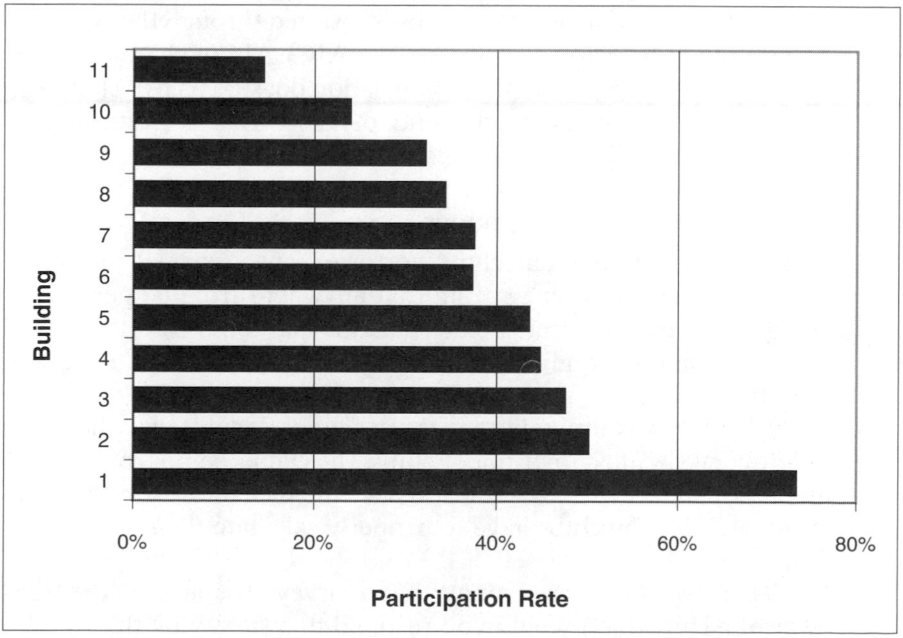

Differences in magnitude usually can be explained by groups having dissimilar education levels, salary levels, or both. People with higher education levels and higher wages are more likely to participate in a 401(k) pension plan. However, this study concerned only librarians, so they all have a relatively similar level of education and wages.

Because librarians are such a homogeneous group, the large variation in participation rates is striking. One explanation for the large differences is the social norms of each building. The social norms of each peer group develop over time. The norms in some buildings included in this study developed to value retirement plans, but in other buildings the norms developed such that participation in the retirement plan is not valued.

INVESTMENT CLUBS

One example of the socialization of investing is the rapid growth of investment clubs. An investment club is a group of family members, friends, or coworkers who have banded together to pool their money and invest it in the stock market. Frequently, the clubs are all men or all women. These groups typically meet once per month and discuss potential stock investments. Every month, the members each contribute some nominal amount ($20 to $100), which is pooled and invested.

The creation of investment clubs is fostered through the National Association of Investors Corporation (NAIC). Although not all clubs are members of the NAIC, the organization boasted 35,810 clubs and 537,150 total members by the end of 2000. This is a substantial increase from the 7,087 clubs registered in 1990.

Investment Club Performance

How do most investment clubs perform? The financial press has made frequent claims suggesting that anywhere from 60 percent to two-thirds of the investment clubs beat the market. If true, this figure would be impressive given that most mutual funds don't routinely beat the market.

However, it is unlikely that these figures accurately reflect the performance of most investment clubs. The claims come from annual surveys of clubs by the NAIC. Consider the problems with this type of survey. First, the clubs have to properly calculate their annualized return.

Second, which clubs respond to the survey? If you were the treasurer of a club, when would you respond to a survey by the NAIC?

You would be far more likely to fill out the survey if your club's returns were high and avoid filling out the survey if the returns were low. The psychological biases of seeking pride and avoiding regret suggest this behavior (see Chapter 3). Indeed, only 5 percent to 10 percent of the clubs return the NAIC survey. It is likely that these are the clubs that calculated a high return. Therefore, the survey results represent only the more successful clubs (at best) and are probably totally misrepresentative of all clubs (at worst).

To get a more objective view of investment club performance, the actual stock holdings of 166 investment clubs using a national discount broker were examined over a 5-year period.[5] As Figure 8.2 shows, the results are not good. During this 5-year period, the Standard & Poor's 500 Index earned an average 18 percent return annually. The clubs averaged a gross return of 17 percent per year. The return net of expenses was only 14.1 percent, so the clubs substantially underperformed the market.

Although media reports suggest that more than 60 percent of the clubs beat the market, it appears that 60 percent actually underperform the market. Indeed, the investing behavior of these clubs shows some of the same characteristics of psychological biases as individuals do. Specifically, trading behavior is consistent with overconfidence (Chapter 2) and the disposition effect (Chapter 3).

FIGURE 8.2 Investment Club Performance Versus Market Performance

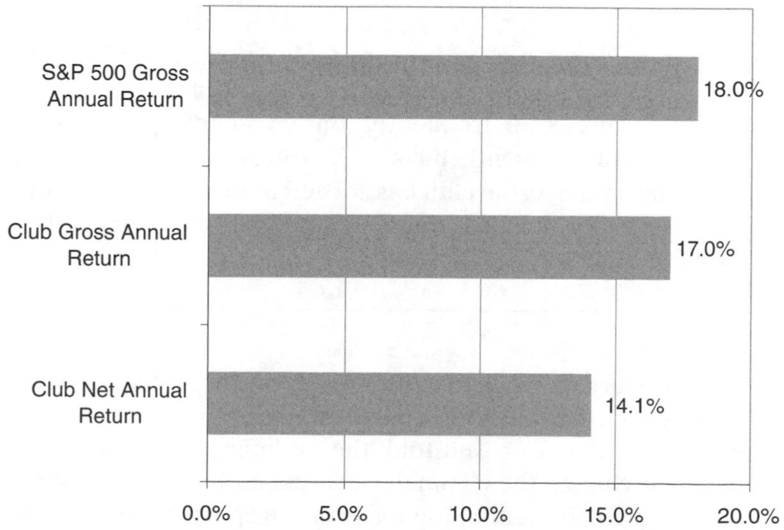

Investment Clubs and Social Dynamics

Although a club's purpose is to create an environment for learning about investing and achieving good returns, most clubs also serve a social purpose; that is, the meetings themselves provide a pretense for family members or friends to get together. Members tend to like the idea of sharing research skills and knowledge about the market while socializing on a regular basis.

The social dynamics of the club play an important role in its investment success. Although some clubs invest as a pretense to socialize, other clubs take their stock picking seriously. For example, the Klondike Investment Club of Buffalo, Wyoming, was rated the number one investment club in America one year by *Value Line*.[6] The 18 members of the club come from all walks of life. Some are young and some are old; some are blue-collar workers and some are white-collar workers, and some have advanced degrees and others are business owners.

What is their secret to success? The Klondikers exercise a high degree of investment formality. For example, this group requires all investment decisions to be made with the help of a rigorous report produced by the sponsoring member. They rely on research, not just stories about a firm. This is important because the approach helps the club avoid some psychological biases. Decisions are based on reason and logic rather than emotion.

Other investment clubs are formed with social interaction as their primary objective. Consider the California Investors Club, which was founded by a group of retired friends who had worked together for many years. Although their social events such as the Christmas party and a day-long golf outing are planned in great detail, their investment decisions are often made without much analysis.[7] Discussion frequently centers on hot tips and speculations; thus, the club frequently buys at the top and later sells at the bottom. As a consequence, the club has earned a poor return. The informality of this club allows each member's psychological biases to combine with the others and be magnified.

THE MEDIA

A large part of our social environment is the media, with various venues and media shows competing for our attention. If the news isn't well written or well told, the audience will pick up a different paper or change the channel. Business and investment writers keep us interested by telling a good story. Reporters also search for the best sound bite to quote. By its very nature, the sound bite is short and catches our attention, but it cannot convey any serious investment analysis; it is designed to convey a story. Most of the time, the media exacerbate our bias toward storytelling and away from formal investment analysis.

Although the media provide us with information and expert opinions, the experts express themselves through one-line explanations and quips. Many of these experts have access to research departments and tremendous analysis tools. Surely, we assume, their opinions are based on significant analysis. However, they rarely talk about the actual analysis, so we get the impression that investment analysis is simply storytelling.

By trying to appeal to our interests and emotions, the media naturally gravitate toward the active investment decisions of stock selection and market timing.

SPEED IS NOT OF THE ESSENCE

If you watch the financial and business news cable channels, you have been bombarded with commercials suggesting that in investing, the slow die first. You need the fastest Internet provider so you can subscribe to the fastest news provider and trade on the fastest online brokerage system. For a while, CNBC even perpetuated this idea by timing and reporting the responsiveness of the major online brokerages.

Making split-second decisions after news reports is not investing; it is trading. Trading is like gambling in that it fosters strong emotional responses. This need for speed magnifies psychological biases.

Consider the simple mistakes that occur when people make split-second decisions. On April 11, 1997, *The Financial Times* ran a story that the Czech Value Fund had invested in fraudulent companies and was facing big losses.[8] When the news reached the United States, the stock with the ticker symbol CVF fell by 32 percent on high volume. The problem was that CVF is the ticker for Castle Convertible Fund, not the Czech Value Fund. By the end of the day, the Castle Fund had mostly recovered, but that doesn't help the investors who sold at the bottom. Other investors' errors can cause you problems.

On June 24, 1998, it was reported that AT&T had agreed to purchase Tele-Communications Inc. for $45.8 billion. The stock with the ticker symbol TCI jumped nearly 5 percent on the news on volume that was more than 37 times normal for the firm.[9] However,

TCI is the ticker symbol for Transcontinental Realty Investors Inc., not Tele-Communications. Interestingly, this had occurred to TCI 5 years earlier when Bell Atlantic Corp. announced its intention to buy Tele-Communications.

A similar case of mistaken identity occurred repeatedly over a 1-year period with people trying to buy MCI Communications on a string of takeover rumors. The New York Stock Exchange stock with the ticker symbol MCI was continually confused with the ticker symbol for MCI Communications, which is MCIC. The MCI ticker symbol is for Massmutual Corporate Investors, a closed-end fund.

The media outlets race to be the first to report these events. Investors then rush to trade on this news with a herd mentality. In this case, the social interaction has influenced people in a way that increases their natural biases.

HERDING

As you learn what other people think about various stocks, the social consensus forms. As people act on this consensus, a herd forms. Investor herding is not unlike that of the antelope. Antelope stay together in herds for protection against predators. One minute the herd is doing nothing, and the next minute the herd is in full gallop. An antelope always has its eyes and ears open so that it knows what the other antelope are doing—it doesn't want to be left behind.

Investors also keep an eye and ear open to what other investors are doing. Many people watch CNBC every day or closely follow chatroom postings on a favorite Web site. Active investors check their portfolio daily. When things start moving, investors everywhere know about it.

The problem with moving with the herd is that it magnifies the psychological biases. It causes one to make decisions that are based on the "feel" of the herd instead of the rigor of formal analysis. In addition, the feeling of regret on picking a loser (Chapter 3) is lower when you know that many others picked the same stock. Misery loves company.

Herding into Stocks

When many investors are influenced by their psychological biases in a common way, a herd forms and the overall market can be affected. This is best illustrated by the irrational exuberance for Internet companies in the late 1990s. Many investors and analysts have been puzzled by the extremely high valuations of Internet firms. For example, when the historical average price/earnings (P/E) ratio of the market is around 15, what was the justification for Yahoo!'s P/E of 1,300 or eBay's P/E of 3,300 in late 1999? Many analysts concluded that new valuation measures were needed for this new revolution in the economy.

Or consider the valuation of eToys,[10] an online toy retailer that went public in 1999. Shortly after the initial public offering, the high price of the stock created a total value of the firm of $8 billion. Typical of Internet companies, eToys had negative earnings of $28.6 million from $30 million in sales. The natural comparison for eToys is Toys "R" Us, the "old economy" leading toy retailer. Even though Toys "R" Us had profits of $376 million, it had a market value of only $6 billion; that is, Toys "R" Us had a lower market valuation than eToys even though it earned 12 times more in profits than eToys had in sales.

This is even more astounding when you realize that the barrier to entry for firms getting on the Web is low. As you might recall, kids started many of the Internet firms on only a shoestring. Indeed, Toys "R" Us quickly developed its own online retail capability, and eToys' market capitalization fell from $8 billion to $29 million.

A Rose.com by Any Other Name

Consider the extent of the herding into Internet companies. One example is the firms that changed their name to FancyNewName.com. Investors went dotcom crazy and scooped up shares of any company related to the Internet. The easiest way to determine whether a firm is related to the Internet is by its name.

Consider the case of Computer Literacy Inc., an online retailer of technology books. This firm changed its name to fatbrain.com because customers kept misspelling (or forgetting) its former Internet address, computerliteracy.com. Note that this firm was already providing its service over the Internet. The change was in name only, not in business strategy. But when word leaked out about the name change, the online stock discussion groups sizzled, and the stock climbed 33 percent in 1 day!

From mid-1998 to mid-1999, a total of 147 publicly traded companies changed to a new name with a dotcom or dotnet ending, or a name that included the word *Internet*.[11] During the 3 weeks after a name change announcement, these firms' stock beat the market by an average of 38 percent. All kinds of firms got in on the action. Some of these firms were already pure Internet companies. They beat the market by 57 percent during the 3 weeks after the name change. Other firms that changed their name had only some Internet experience. These firms earned 35 percent over the market. Some firms that changed their name were changing from a non-Internet to an Internet focus and beat the market by 16 percent. In fact, even firms with little or no Internet experience changed their names and enjoyed the large stock price increases. These firms had a non-Internet core business, and no evidence was available to show that these firms had the expertise or experience to be successful. Yet, Net-crazy traders bid up their stock prices to such a degree that they beat the market by 48 percent. These huge increases in stock price did not diminish over the following 3 months. Investors appeared to be eager to throw money at Internet companies.

SHORT-TERM FOCUS

In active trading, your thoughts are more like those of a trader than an investor. Instead of buying a stock because you think the company's products, market share, and management will dominate in the future, you buy a stock because you think the price will rise in the next week, day, or hour. The firm's products, market share, and management become ancillary, or even irrelevant. Take Sharon, for example, who was interviewed by the PBS show *Frontline*.[12] She invested her family's entire life savings into two tiny technology stocks, placing most of it in one firm. "To tell you the truth, I don't even know the name of it. I know the call letters are AMLN. It's supposed to double by August," she said. For the record, AMLN is the ticker symbol for Amylin Pharmaceuticals.

Faith

"Things are different this time. The old valuation measures are no longer appropriate." These are the types of comments that are often uttered during a period of extreme herding because the high prices cannot be justified with traditional measures. When the scale says you have gained 30 pounds, the problem is obvious your scale no longer works. While investing with the herd, people invest on the basis of faith, not due diligence.

Social Validation

People want to talk about investing. Conversation about investments becomes popular at social occasions, and the online discussion groups heat up. The expansion of radio talk shows featuring investment discussions and the call-in questions to CNBC demonstrate how investing invades other parts of life.

Herding and overvaluation do not occur because of new economics or new technologies—they occur because of human psychology. New economics and new technology are only the rallying cry for the herd. When overconfidence (see Chapter 2) is combined with emotions, a problem results. The problem is magnified when everyone is caught up in making psychology-based decisions.

Questions

1. How does one's level of social interaction influence the likelihood of investing in the stock market and the type of stocks purchased?
2. Give examples of investment club environments in which psychological biases are exacerbated. Give examples of environments or tools that help control the biases.
3. How did the media influence investors in the late 1990s to herd into marginal firms?

End Notes

1. These figures originate from the Survey of Consumer Finances as reported by C. Bertaut and M. Sarr-McCluer, "Household Portfolios in the U.S," Board of Governors of the Federal Reserve working paper, 2000.
2. Robert Shiller and John Pound, "Survey Evidence on Diffusion of Interest and Information Among Investors," *Journal of Economic Behavior and Organization* 12(1989): 47–66.
3. Harrison Hong, Jeffrey D. Kubik, and Jeremy C. Stein, "Social Interaction and Stock-Market Participation," *Journal of Finance* (forthcoming, Feb. 2004).
4. Esther Duflo and Emmanuel Saez, "Participation and Investment Decisions in a Retirement Plan: The Influence of Colleagues' Choices," *Journal of Public Economics* 85(2002): 121–148.
5. Brad M. Barber and Terrance Odean, "Too Many Cooks Spoil the Profits: Investment Club Performance," *Financial Analysts Journal* (Jan./Feb. 2000): 17–25.
6. Tony Cook, "Six Moneymaking Lessons You Can Learn from America's Top Investing Club," *Money Magazine* 25(Dec. 1996): 88–93.
7. Brooke Harrington, *Capital and Community: Investment Clubs and Stock Market Populism*, Cambridge University Press (in press).
8. "Czech Markets Watchdog Chief Forced to Quit," *Financial Times,* April 11, 1997, page 3.
9. Michael S. Rashes, "Massively Confused Investors Making Conspicuously Ignorant Choices (MCI-MCIC)," *Journal of Finance* 56(2001): 1911–1927.
10. Andrew Edgecliffe, "eToys Surges After Listing," *Financial Times,* May 21, 1999, page 29.
11. Michael Cooper, Orlin Dimitrov, and Raghavendra Rau, "A Rose.com by Any Other Name," *Journal of Finance* 56(2001): 2371–2388.
12. "Frontline," *Stock Market*, January 4, 1997.

CHAPTER 9

Emotion and Investment Decisions

Traditional finance theory assumes that people make rational decisions to maximize their wealth in the face of risk and uncertainty. Because money is involved, reason and logic will overcome emotion and psychological biases, it would seem. Is this a good assumption? In reality, the situation might be just the opposite. Emotion might overcome reason when one is making a risky decision.

FEELINGS AND DECISIONS

Psychologists and economists who have examined the role of emotions in decision making have found that unrelated feelings and emotions can affect decisions.[1] The term *unrelated* in this case means emotions that are not attributed to the decision. For example, you might be in a good mood because the sun is shining or because your favorite team just won. This good feeling can subsequently influence an investment decision. Emotions interact with the cognitive evaluation process to eventually lead to a decision. At times, emotional reactions diverge from reason and logic to dominate the decision-making process. Indeed, the more complex and uncertain a situation is, the more emotions influence a decision.[2]

The central question then becomes this: What is the relative importance of emotion and reason in decision making? It appears that emotions play a large role. For example, neurologist Antonio Damasio reported on patients who suffered damage to the ventromedial frontal cortices of the brain. This damage leaves intelligence, memory, and capacity for logic intact but impairs the ability to feel. Through various experiments, it has been surmised that the lack of emotion in the decision-making process destroys the ability to make rational decisions.[3] Indeed, these people become socially dysfunctional. Damasio concluded that emotion is an integral component of making reasonable decisions.

Consider how psychologists study the effect of moods on decisions. They have their subjects write an essay about a sad or happy event in their lives. Reliving the event through their writing puts the subjects in bad or good moods, respectively. This mood appears to affect their predictions about the future. People who are in a bad mood are more pessimistic about the future than people who are in a good mood. That is, the subjects who are in a good mood give a higher probability of good things happening and a lower probability of bad things happening.

In one study, the people who were in a good mood believed they had an 84 percent chance that "Within the next year, I will meet a new person who will come to be a very good friend."[4] The people who were in a bad mood believed that the chance of this happening was only 51 percent. Alternatively, when asked for the probability that "I will be involved in a major automobile accident within the next 5 years," people who were in a bad mood thought the chance was 52 percent, and those who were in a good mood thought the chance was only 23 percent. People who are in a good mood view the future differently than people who are in a bad mood.

In addition to the importance of emotion, people are often insensitive to changes in the facts used in cognition. One such fact is the probability of outcomes. For example, people tend to treat the probability of winning a lottery of 1 in 10 million or 1 in 10,000 similarly when making a decision. Yet, one has a 1,000 times higher chance of happening. In particular, the decision to take a gamble is relatively insensitive to large changes in probability when the gamble evokes strong emotions. In short, emotions drive the process of complex decision making.

FEELINGS AND FINANCE

Financial decisions are complex and include risk and uncertainty. Thus, background feelings, or mood, may influence financial decisions. This is called the *misattribution bias*. That is, people often misattribute the mood they are in to the financial decision at hand. If someone is in a good mood, he or she is more likely to be optimistic in evaluating an investment. Good (bad) moods will increase (decrease) the likelihood of investing in risky assets, like stocks. The misattribution bias has been examined in financial decisions in several ways.

Feelings Affect Investment Decisions

Consider that an investor's decision to buy or sell a stock is based on expectations. The traditional finance view is embodied by the rational expectations model, which assumes that investor expectations are derived from using tools such as fundamental analysis and modern portfolio theory. These tools require making certain assumptions about the future. What growth rate will the firm achieve over the next 3 years? What are its expected return, expected variance, and expected correlation with other assets? Even the most sophisticated investors do not agree about which methods produce the most accurate assumptions. The rational expectations model requires that investors resolve these uncertainties in an unbiased and rational way. Yet, evidence indicates that people make biased and nonrational choices, driven by emotion and cognitive errors.

Indeed, even those investors who use quantitative methods such as fundamental analysis must include educated guesswork about some assumptions. Some fundamental analysis techniques are more sophisticated than others, but they all involve assumptions about the future. To illustrate, consider the constant discount rate model taught to finance students around the world, $PV = D_1 / (k-g)$. Investors must estimate the constant growth rate, g. Given the influence of mood on risky and uncertain decisions, the expected value of the growth rate may become biased. In turn, this biases the value computed in the model.

For this example, assume that the annual return, k, is known to be 11 percent, and there will be a long-term dividend growth rate of 5 percent. An investor who is in a good mood might optimistically overestimate the growth rate to be 7 percent. This would cause the investor to believe the stock is worth 50 percent more than the belief of an unbiased investor. The optimistic investor might purchase the stock thinking it is undervalued, when in reality it is not.

Sunshine

For the past several decades, psychologists have been documenting how the sun affects our decisions. A lack of sunlight has been linked to depression and even suicide. Without the sun, we feel bad. When the sun is shinning, we feel good. This good mood makes us optimistic about our future prospects and affects our decision-making process.

Even our financial decisions may be affected by sunshine. For example, you will probably leave a bigger tip for your server at lunch if it is sunny outside. You do not even need to be outside to feel good about sunshine. One psychologist conducted an experiment at a large hotel where many of the rooms did not have windows.[5] When a guest from one of these interior rooms ordered room service, the server would mention the weather outside. The server received an average tip of 18.8 percent on rainy days. This increased to 24.4 percent on cloudy days, 26.4 percent on partially sunny days, and 29.4 percent on sunny days. People give a tip that is more than 50 percent higher on sunny days than on rainy days.

Can the happy mood of a sunny day affect investors and the stock market? If the sunshine puts investors in a good mood, they will be more optimistic about future prospects. Therefore, investors are more likely to buy stock than to sell stock on sunny days. If the tendency to buy rather than sell affects enough investors, the stock market itself could be affected. Two financial economists examined this possibility by looking at stock market returns and the weather in the financial cities of the world.[6] Specifically, they compared the daily return in 26 stock exchanges around the world to the weather in the 26 cities in which the stock markets are located.

These researchers used a weather scale with nine levels ranging from completely sunny to completely miserable. They found that the daily returns for sunny days are higher than the daily returns for nonsunny days. Indeed, the returns for the sunniest days are much higher than the returns for the most miserable days of weather. When they annualized the difference between the sunniest and worst days in all 26 cities, they found that sunny days outperform miserable weather days by 24.6 percent per year.

The annualized difference in returns between sunny and miserable days is shown for several cities in Figure 9.1. The average for all 26 cities is also shown. Note that sunny days outperform on the New York Stock Exchange to the tune of 15 percent per year. Sunny days earn an annualized return over miserable days in London of 22.1 percent, Copenhagen of 4.1 percent, and Paris of 19.7 percent. Not every day is sunny or miserable; most days are in between. However, this illustrates that the sun affects investors and the market.

Another way to examine the effect of sunshine on investor mood and behavior is to examine stock market returns by seasons. Psychologists have found that the decreasing amount of daylight during the fall and winter leads to depression for many people. This depression is called seasonal affective disorder (SAD). It is believed that 10 million Americans are afflicted with SAD and another 15 million suffer from a mild case of "winter blues." Remember that people who are in a bad mood or in a depressed state are more critical and

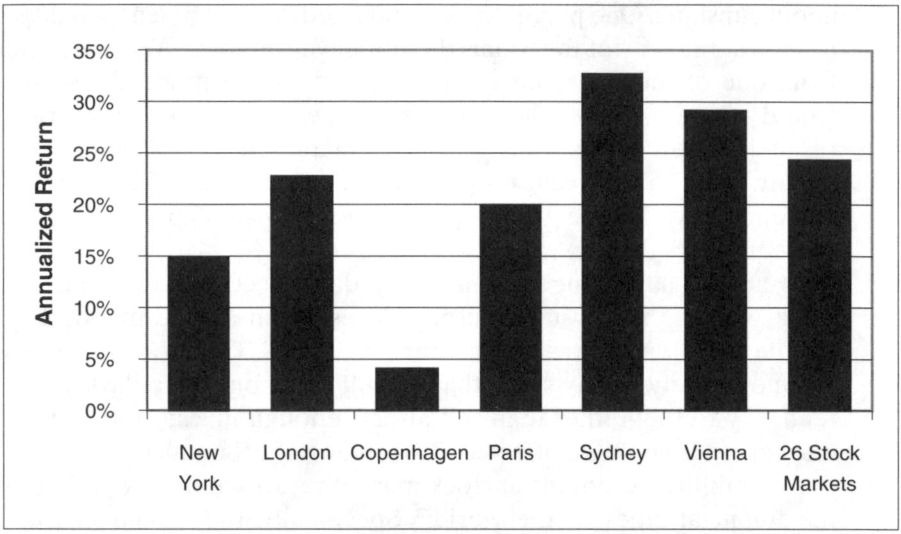

FIGURE 9.1 Annualized Difference in Return Between Sunny Days and Miserable Weather Days for Stock Markets Around the World

pessimistic, and people who are in a good mood are more optimistic. This leads to greater risk taking by people who are in good moods than by people who are in bad moods.

If the decreasing length of daylight affects many investors, they will take less risk. Three financial economists investigated this possibility by studying seven stock markets around the world: Australia, Great Britain, Canada, Germany, New Zealand, Sweden, and the United States.[7] They found that stock returns are lower during the fall when daylight decreases until December 21, the longest night of the year. This effect is strongest for stock markets that are furthest away from the equator (Sweden and Great Britain). Also consistent with this idea is that the effect occurs during the spring for markets in the southern hemisphere (Australia and New Zealand). Again, it appears that daylight (or the lack of it) affects our mood. This mood also affects our investment decisions, our decision-making process, and the amount of risk we are willing to take.

Optimism

Optimism skews a person's beliefs and judgments. Optimistic people believe they are less likely than average to experience disease and divorce, or to be a victim of crime. This belief can cause the optimist to take unnecessary risks.

Consider the average cigarette smoker. The fact that smoking is hazardous to your health comes as no surprise to smokers. Warnings are printed on every pack and on TV commercials. Everyone knows that smoking increases the risk of lung cancer, but smokers optimistically believe they personally are at low risk for the disease. After all, you would not be very intelligent if you thought you were at high risk and smoked anyway. To help preserve one's self-image of being intelligent, smokers are optimistic about their chance of getting lung cancer, which allows them to continue a hazardous behavior.

Investors who are in a good mood can also suffer from optimistic decisions; that is, investors can also believe that nothing bad is likely to happen to their stock picks. Optimism affects investors in two ways. First, optimistic investors tend to do less critical analysis in making their stock decisions. Second, optimists tend to ignore (or downplay) negative information about their stocks. In other words, the optimistic investor holds fast to the beliefs that a firm is great, even when negative news comes out about the firm—just as the smoker downplays the risk of getting cancer after reading the warning label.

Consider the circumstances surrounding the news of a potential breakthrough in the development of a cure for cancer by EntreMed (ticker symbol ENMD).[8] The biotechnology company reported a major breakthrough in the process of developing resistance-free cancer therapy in the trade publication *Nature*.[9] EntreMed had the rights to commercialize the potentially cancer-curing process. A media blitz on the finding was kicked off with a May 3, 1998, front-page article in the *New York Times*.[10] The stock's price quadrupled the next day.

In the months preceding this announcement, EntreMed's stock traded at about $12 per share. After the *New York Times* article, the price quickly jumped to more than $50 per share and then settled into a price of about $31. Certainly, owning the rights to a cure for cancer is something to be optimistic about. This is a story that could have a big impact on many people as well as your investments. However, this news wasn't new. The report in *Nature* and other media attention had previously occurred in November 1997. The original attention had moved the stock price from about $12 per share to more than $15. The price had then fallen back to $12 per share when the second round of media attention occurred. See the price graph of EntreMed in Figure 9.2.

Are the rights to a potential cancer cure worth a $30-per-share stock price when the previous stock price was $12? Those rights probably are worth the increase. However, this story became more interesting on November 12, 1998, when the *Wall Street Journal*

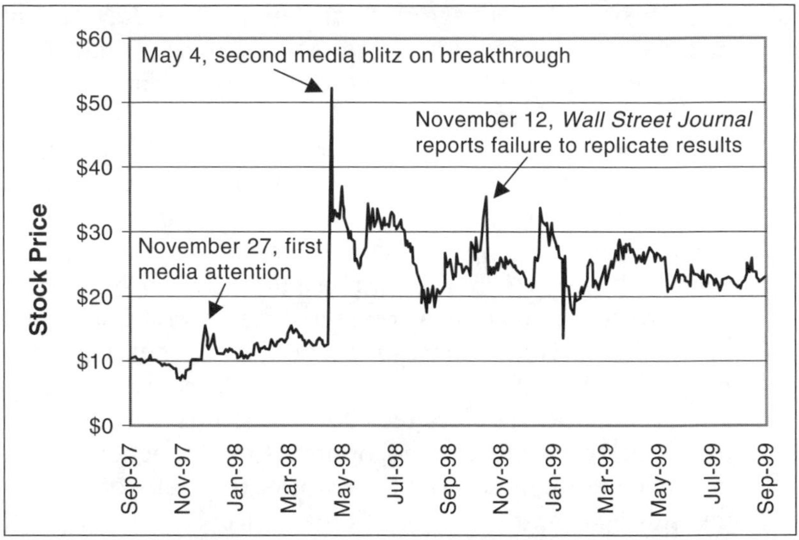

FIGURE 9.2 Price of EntreMed During Period of Cancer Breakthrough Announcements

(WSJ) reported that other laboratories failed to replicate the results of EntreMed.[11] That is, EntreMed had the rights to a process that did not cure cancer after all. The news took the price from $35 per share down to $22 per share. Even a year later, the stock was still trading at about $22 per share.

If EntreMed was worth $12 per share before the breakthrough announcement and $31 per share after the announcement, is it worth $22 per share after learning that the procedure didn't work after all? It seems that the stock should be worth no more than the preannouncement price of $12 per share. However, once investors get optimistic, they tend to discount (or ignore) negative news. In this case, the negative news is pertinent to the prospects of the firm. By discounting its importance, investors did not make the best decisions. It frequently takes a while for the optimism to wear off. In this case, it took nearly 3 years for EntreMed's stock price to fall back below $12 per share.

The price of a stock is frequently set by the optimistic investors. If many investors are optimistic about a stock and many are pessimistic, the price of the stock will be driven by the optimists. This is because the pessimists stay on the sideline while the optimists buy. The optimists drive up the stock price with their buying. This makes the pessimists even more pessimistic, but staying on the sideline does not affect the price. A stock will have a large number of optimists and pessimists (as opposed to mostly neutral-bias investors) when there is a large degree of uncertainty about the prospects of the stock. The prospects of large, well-established firms have less uncertainty, so their stocks prices are generally more reflective of actual prospects than of optimistic prospects. For example, the business potential of General Motors, Procter & Gamble, and Intel are pretty well-known and leave little room for a high degree of optimism and pessimism. For firms with a high degree of uncertainty, optimists tend to set the stock price until that uncertainty is resolved. This resolution usually includes a downward revision of optimism and a decline in the stock price.

Rampant Optimism and Irrational Exuberance

Rampant optimism, or irrational exuberance, can be found in the stock market. Consider the case of Palm and 3Com. 3Com was a profitable firm that sold computer network systems and services. One of the products it developed in its Palm subsidiary was the handheld computer known as the Palm Pilot. 3Com decided to spin off Palm into its own company. The plan was to issue 4 percent of the shares of Palm in an initial public offering (IPO), sell 1 percent of the shares to a consortium of firms, and distribute the remaining 95 percent of the Palm shares to 3Com stockholders. On March 2, 2000, 3Com sold the 5 percent of Palm in the IPO. The other 95 percent of the Palm stock was to be distributed later in the year as 1.5 shares of Palm for every 1 share of 3Com stock owned. So if you owned 1 share of 3Com stock, after the distribution you would own 1.5 shares of Palm and still own 1 share of 3Com.

By the end of the IPO day, the newly issued shares of Palm traded at $95.06. Because one share of 3Com would receive 1.5 shares of Palm, the 3Com stock should have been worth a minimum of $142.59 (this is equal to 1.5 × $95.06) from the value of the Palm shares alone. 3Com's non-Palm operations also had value. These businesses were earning $750 million in annual profits for 3Com,[12] so the 3Com stock price should have been much higher than $142.59. However, 3Com stock closed at only $81.81 per share that day.

If you wanted to own Palm stock, you could have bought 3Com stock and gotten the Palm stock for an effective price of $54.54 (which is equal to $81.81/1.5) per share and owned the 3Com stock for free. Either 3Com stock was priced too low or Palm stock was priced too high. Because 3Com was a larger, better-established firm and Palm was a new firm in an uncertain environment, it is likely that optimistic investors affected the Palm stock. All relevant information about Palm and 3Com was readily available before the IPO. The day after the IPO, the *Wall Street Journal* and the *New York Times* ran articles highlighting the strange mispricing. Yet, the mispricing continued for months. The value of the embedded Palm stock in the 3Com stock continued to be worth more than the 3Com stock itself for 2 more months (until May 9). Again, optimistic investors ignored, or minimized, bad news about their firms.

Although the 3Com/Palm example is interesting, it is not unique. For example, HNC Software spun off Retek on November 17, 1999; Daisytek spun off PFSWeb on December 1, 1999; and Methode Electronics spun off Stratos Lightwave on June 26, 2000. In all three cases, optimistic investors drove the new company's stock price up. Just like 3Com and Palm, the price of the parent company's stock was less than the embedded value of the spin-off firm's stock price. These three other cases shared another thing with 3Com and Palm. In each case, the new company's stock price fell by 50 percent or more during the ensuing 6 months.

Other similar examples can be cited. Some companies do not entirely spin off a new company. That is, sometimes the parent company will keep some stock of the subsidiary instead of distributing it to the shareholders. The optimism about the subsidiary can get so great that the price gets run up and mispricing results between the parent and the subsidiary. For example, in September 1999, Flowers Industries owned 55 percent of the shares of Keebler Foods. The stock price of Keebler was such that its total market capitalization (number of shares of stock times the stock price) was $2.50 billion. Because Flowers owned 55 percent of Keebler, its ownership was worth $1.38 billion, yet the total market capitalization of Flowers was only $1.36 billion. Flowers's stock price was such that its market capitalization was lower than the holdings of just one of its assets, Keebler. The value of the other assets was approximately $1 billion. Clearly, either Keebler was severely overpriced or Flowers was underpriced. This phenomenon has occurred to several firms and illustrates the price inflation of stocks driven by optimism.[13] Buying a stock whose price is driven up by optimism usually leads to losses as the optimism unwinds—and eventually, the optimism always unwinds.

This investor mania caused a price bubble in the 1990s. In the year 2000, the bubble burst. The technology-laden NASDAQ Composite stock index experienced a 54 percent decline from its peak in March to its low in December 2000. Internet-focused stock indexes such as the TSC Internet Sector Index declined by 79 percent over the same period. In comparison, the Dow Jones Industrial Average increased by 4 percent.

MARKET BUBBLES

The more things change, the more *people* stay the same. Market bubbles are not a recent phenomenon, nor are they uncommon.

One of the most impressive market bubbles occurred in Holland in the 1630s.[14] What makes that bubble so amusing is that the highly sought-after commodity was the tulip bulb. Over a 5-year period, tulip bulb mania inflated bulb prices to the point where one bulb was worth 10 times a yoke of oxen. A tulip bulb costing nearly $100,000? Then an out-of-town sailor inadvertently popped the tulip bulb price bubble. Mistaking the bulb for an onion, he ate it. Wondering whether the bulbs were worth the high prices, panic erupted; within a week, the bulbs were almost worthless.

Modern market bubbles have common elements. Given the statement that follows, how would you fill in the blank?

> We are in a new era. __________ has ushered in a new type of economy. Those stuck in the old ways will quickly fall away. Traditional company valuation techniques do not capture the value of this revolution.

You probably answered "the Internet." However, if you lived in 1850, you would have said "the railroad." If you lived in the 1920s, you might have said "the Federal Reserve System" or "the radio." In the mid-1950s, the answer would have been "the New Deal." Even as recently as 1990, you might have said "biotechnology." In each case, this rationalization accompanied a great bull market and preceded a great decline. The point is that price bubbles are not uncommon, nor is each one unique.

SUMMARY

Emotions are an important part of the decision-making process. This is especially true for decisions that involve a high degree of uncertainty, such as investment decisions. Sometimes, emotion can overcome logic in this process. Too much optimism leads investors to underestimate risk and overestimate expected performance. Optimistic investors tend to seek good-story stocks and be less critical. Pessimistic investors tend to be more analytical. Extended, extreme optimism can cause price bubbles.

Questions

1. How might being in a good mood or bad mood influence an investor's decisions?
2. How can optimism and pessimism affect the results of quantitative asset pricing?
3. Explain the misattribution bias and its effect on investment behavior.

End Notes

1. For example, see George Loewenstein, Elki U. Weber, Christopher K. Hsee, and Ned Welch, "Risk as Feelings," *Psychological Bulletin* 127(2001): 267–286; and Paul Slovic, Melissa Finucane, Ellen Peters, and Donald MacGregor, "The Affect Heuristic" in *Heuristics and Biases: The Psychology of Intuitive Judgment*, edited by T. Gilovich, D. Griffin, and D. Kahneman, New York: Cambridge University Press, 2002: 397–420.
2. Joseph P. Forgas, "Mood and Judgment: The Affect Infusion Model (AIM)," *Psychological Bulletin* 117(1995): 39–66.
3. Antonio Damasio, *Descartes' Error: Emotion, Reason, and the Human Brain,* New York: Avon, 1994; Antonio Damasio, D. Tranel, and H. Damasio, "Individuals with Sociopathic Behavior Caused by Frontal Damage Fail to Respond Autonomically to Social Stimul," *Behavioral Brain Research* 41(1990): 81–94.
4. William Wright and Gordon Bower, "Mood Effects on Subjective Probability Assessment," *Organizational Behavior and Human Decision Processes* 52(1992): 276–291.
5. Bruce Rind, "Effect of Beliefs About Weather Conditions on Tipping," *Journal of Applied Social Psychology* 26(1996): 137–147.
6. David Hirshleifer and Tyler Shumway, "Good Day Sunshine: Stock Returns and the Weather," *Journal of Finance* 58(2003): 1009–1032.
7. Mark Kamstra, Lisa Kramer, and Maurice Levi, "Winter Blues: A Sad Stock Market Cycle," *American Economic Review* 93(2003): 324–343.
8. For more details of this event, see Gur Huberman and Tomer Regev, "Contagious Speculation and a Cure for Cancer: A Nonevent That Made Stock Prices Soar," *Journal of Finance* 56(2001): 387–396.
9. Thomas Boehm, Judah Folkman, Timothy Browder, and Michael O'Reilly, "Antiangiogenic Therapy of Experimental Cancer Does Not Induce Acquired Drug Resistance," *Nature* 390(1997): 401–407.
10. Gina Kolata, "Hope in the Lab: A Special Report; A Cautious Awe Greets Drugs That Eradicate Tumors in Mice," *New York Times*, May 3, 1998, page 1.
11. Ralph King, "Novel Cancer Approach from Noted Scientist Hits Stumbling Block," *Wall Street Journal*, Nov. 12, 1998, page A1.
12. For additional discussion, see Brad Barber and Terrance Odean, "The Internet and the Investor," *Journal of Economic Perspectives* 15(2001): 41–54.
13. Bradford Cornell and Qiao Liu, "The Parent Company Puzzle: When Is the Whole Worth Less Than One of the Parts?" *Journal of Corporate Finance* 7(2001): 341–366.
14. Robert Sobel, *The Big Board: A History of the New York Stock Market*, New York: The Free Press, 1965.

CHAPTER 10

Self-Control and Decision Making

Three years of losses often turn investors with 30-year horizons into investors with 3-year horizons; they want out.

KENNETH FISHER AND MEIR STATMAN[1]

A common adage on Wall Street is that the markets are motivated by two emotions: fear and greed. Indeed, this textbook suggests that investors are affected by these emotions. However, acting on these emotions is rarely the wise move. The decision that benefits investors over the long term is usually made in the absence of strong emotions. In fact, investors face a lifelong struggle between decisions that make the present more enjoyable and ones that make the future more enjoyable. Many decisions require balancing this trade-off. "Do I read this chapter now or later?" "Do I purchase a new stereo or invest the money for the future?"

Richard Thaler and Hersh Shefrin describe the self-control problem as the interaction between a person's two selfs: the planner and the doer.[2] The doer wishes to consume now instead of later and procrastinates on unpleasant tasks. The planner wishes to save for later consumption and complete unpleasant tasks now. This conflict between desire and willpower occurs because people are influenced by long-term rational concerns and by more short-term emotional factors.

Fortunately, people recognize the fact that they are susceptible to weak willpower and spur-of-the moment decisions. Our society is full of examples of people who recognize that they need help with self-control. Common examples are those who utilize dietary clinics, Alcoholics Anonymous, drug-abuse groups, and similar organizations.

SHORT-TERM VERSUS LONG-TERM FOCUS

People like to receive rewards early and put off unpleasant tasks. However, this attitude depends on the circumstances. Consider the following example.[3] If people are asked on February 1 whether they would prefer to do 7 hours of an unpleasant task on April 1 or 8 hours of the unpleasant task on April 15, people will say they would prefer to do the lesser amount of work on April 1. However, if given the same choice on the morning of April 1, most people will decide to delay the work until April 15, even though it means doing more total work. When making decisions involving the present, people often procrastinate, even when it causes more work later.

This attitude also can affect investment decisions. For example, most people would rather get $50 immediately than $100 in 2 years, foregoing a 41 percent annual return. Alternatively, almost no one prefers $50 in 4 years to $100 in 6 years even though this is the same choice, albeit 4 years into the future.[4] People seem to view the present differently from how they view the future. This leads to strong desire and weak willpower.

CONTROLLING YOURSELF

Most people want to maintain self-control and implement decisions that provide benefits over the long-term. However, they often recognize that their desire is stronger than their willpower is. Therefore, people use many techniques to help strengthen their willpower. I categorize these techniques into two groups: rules of thumb and environment control.[5] These techniques help people reduce desire and increase willpower.

People implement rules of thumb to control their behavior. They rationally create these rules in the absence of emotions during times when willpower is high. During situations filled with high emotion and desire, people rely on these rules to remind them how to exert willpower. Consider these common rules.

- People control spending by—fighting the urge to splurge.
- Recovering alcoholics use—not one drop.
- Retired people control spending by the rule—don't touch the principle.
- Employees contribute to their 401(k) plan by the rule—save much, don't touch.

- Investors try to control trading behavior with—buy low, sell high.
- Investors try to maintain a long-term perspective during bear markets with—stay the course.

People also control their environment to help with willpower. Common ways to control the environment are to remove desired objects from the area or avoid situations that are likely to cause self-control problems. Common examples include the following.

- People on a diet will not keep cookies in the house.
- Gambling addicts will avoid going to Las Vegas.
- People who are always late set their watches a few minutes fast.
- People who have trouble getting out of bed place the alarm clock across the room to force themselves to get up.

People are often willing to incur costs in order to maintain self-control. For example, professional athletes earn the vast majority of their income during a short time period. After earning millions of dollars, some end up bankrupt because they were unable to control their desire to spend. To help with willpower, some athletes hire agents to impose limits on their consumption.

As another example, consider the average smoker. Most smokers recognize that they should not smoke too much (or at all). In order to limit their smoking, most smokers buy cigarettes by the pack. Purchasing cigarettes by the carton is much cheaper; however, the easiest way to control the number of cigarettes smoked is to control the number available. Although this technique is more expensive, smokers are willing to pay the extra cost in order to control their environment in the pursuit of stronger willpower.

SAVING AND SELF-CONTROL

Saving for retirement is difficult because it requires self-control. In 1971, 51 percent of retirees had no income from financial assets. Only 22 percent of the retirees earned investment income that amounted to more than 20 percent of their total income. Most retirees succumbed to the desire for current consumption during their peak earning years and procrastinated when it came to saving for the future.[6]

People find it psychologically easier to save from a lump-sum payment than from regular income.[7] Consider two people who each earn $25,000 per year. The first earns the $25,000 as 12 monthly payments.

The second person earns $20,000 in 12 monthly payments and then receives a $5,000 bonus paid all at once. Assuming that both wage earners incur the equivalent amount in expenses, they should save the same amount for retirement. However, it is more likely that the person with the bonus will save more. Coming up with the disposable income to save is easier with a lump-sum payment (or cash windfall). Saving money from a monthly salary requires much more self-control.[8] This might be why the savings rate of countries like Japan is higher than that of the United States. A higher percentage of income in Japan is from the year-end bonus. However, a simple environmental control of automatic payroll deduction or an automatic investment plan can make saving easier.

This also explains people's propensity for giving interest-free loans to the government; that is, most people overpay their taxes throughout the year and then receive a tax refund in the spring. In 1996, approximately 76 percent of individual taxpayers overpaid their taxes an aggregate of $117 billion. That is a lot of foregone interest.

People can easily adjust their withholding rate and retain more of their income during the year. However, many prefer to overpay. In an experiment using MBA students and a case of a hypothetical wager earner, 43 percent of the 132 students chose to pay more than the minimum required quarterly tax payment.[9] People recognize that a $50 increase in their monthly income is likely to be spent. They know they are more likely to save the equivalent, a $600 refund.

401(k) AND IRA PLANS

The Individual Retirement Account (IRA) and the corporate 401(k) pension plan are two savings innovations that have helped people save and invest for the future. These plans are simple to implement and provide an immediate tax reduction. In addition, the large penalties for early withdrawal add the incentive needed to keep the money invested for retirement. Most people who invest in an IRA or a 401(k) plan contribute again the following year.[10] That is, they form a habit to help their willpower.

It is clearly rational to contribute to an IRA. The investment earnings in an IRA grow tax deferred because no income or capital gains taxes are paid on the profits each year. Instead, income taxes are paid on the money that is withdrawn from the IRA in retirement. Therefore, it is best to contribute the money to the IRA as soon as possible to let it grow tax-deferred for as long as possible. To get the tax deduction for the 2004 tax year, you should contribute on

January 1, 2004, to get the maximum time benefit of the money growing. However, people do not have the self-control to invest early in the year. The tax laws allow contributions made as late as April 15, 2005, to count as a 2004 tax-year IRA. Indeed, most taxpayers who contribute to an IRA will not contribute until 2005 for their 2004 IRA.[11] They need the deadline to exert self-control.

Contributing to your 401(k) plan is also considered the smart thing to do. However, since the inception of the 401(k), the most difficult aspect for plan administrators has been getting employees to begin contributing because people procrastinate. The more important the decision is, the more likely people are to procrastinate.[12] Employees often believe they can make a better decision if they just take a little more time to analyze the choices. The continuous delay costs the employee the two most important factors in building a retirement nest egg: time and invested capital.

The problem is getting worse because companies are increasing the number of options available in their 401(k) plans. These plans started with three or four choices (typically company stock, money market, bond fund, and stock fund). However, many plans now adopt mutual fund families with hundreds of different funds to select from. Having more options available induces more procrastination. In order to help employees with self-control, some companies now automatically sign up employees for contributions when they are first hired. That way, although the employee procrastinates on how to change the automatic contribution defaults, he or she is still contributing and investing.

SELF-CONTROL AND DIVIDENDS

A long-standing puzzle in traditional finance has been why individuals have a strong preference for cash dividends. This is especially puzzling considering that dividend income is taxed at a higher marginal rate than capital gains.

Consider the example demonstrated in Table 10.1. An investor owns 1,000 shares of a $100 stock for a total value of $100,000. If the stock pays a 1 percent dividend, then the investor receives $1,000 and the stock price falls to $99 per share. The 1,000 shares are now worth $99,000 because the investment paid out 1 percent of its value. The decrease in the stock price is the amount of the dividend paid. However, if the investor owes 20 percent in dividend tax, he keeps only $800 after taxes. In sum, the investor ends up with $800 in cash and stock worth $99,000.

TABLE 10.1 Real Dividends Versus Homemade Dividends

	Receive Dividend	*Homemade Dividend*
Starting Number of Shares Owned	1,000	1,000
Beginning Price Per Share	$100	$100
Beginning Stock Value	$100,000	$100,000
Per Share Dividend	$1	$0
Pre-tax Dividend Income	$1,000	
Dividend by Selling 10 Shares		
Selling Shares Pre-tax Income		$1,000
Ending Number of Shares	1,000	990
Price Per Share	$99	$100
Ending Stock Value	$99,000	$99,000
Taxes		
Dividend Tax (20% rate)	$200	$0
Capital Gains Tax (20% rate, 50% gain)	$0	$100
After Tax Income	$800	$900

Now consider the alternative. Assume that the stock does not pay a dividend. If the investor wants some cash, he must create his own dividend by selling 10 shares at $100 per share to receive the $1,000 in proceeds. This is called a homemade dividend. The investor is now left with 990 shares of a stock worth $100 each for a total of $99,000. If the stock sold has no capital gains liability, then the investor owes no taxes and keeps the entire $1,000 in cash. Note that the investor is better off creating his own dividend. If the stock had a cost basis of $50 per share and capital gains are taxed at 20 percent, then $100 is owed in taxes. The investor is still better off making his own dividends.

The investor who wishes to maximize wealth and cash flow should seek income through homemade dividends rather than cash dividends. However, people generally prefer cash dividends. This behavior is irrational in traditional finance but can be explained by investor psychology.

Mental accounting causes investors to separate investments into different mental accounts. In investing for the income mental account, investors buy high-dividend stocks, bonds, and annuities. A different mental account is used for capital gains.

These mental accounts are especially useful for investors who need to exert self-control. A retired person may recognize that her wealth needs to outlive her; that is, she doesn't want to outlive her money. Because she might be tempted to spend too much money, she enacts a common rule of thumb to help her with self-control: Never touch the principle. This rule is a helpful reminder to avoid overspending. However, it can also inhibit the kind of creative thinking that increases income, such as the use of homemade dividends.

BEATING THE BIASES

Many biases have been discussed in this book. This section suggests strategies for overcoming the psychological biases.

Strategy 1: Understand the Biases

This is the purpose of the previous eight chapters of this textbook. Recognizing the biases in yourself and in others is an important step in avoiding them.

Strategy 2: Know Why You Are Investing

Many investors largely overlook this simple step of the investing process. Most people have only some vague notion of their investment goals. "I want a lot of money so I can travel abroad when I retire." "I want to make the money to send my kids to college." Sometimes people think of vague goals in a negative form. "I don't want to be poor when I retire." These vague notions do little to provide investment direction, nor do they help you avoid the psychological biases that inhibit good decision making.

Establishing specific goals and ways to meet them is important. Instead of a vague notion of wanting to travel after retirement, define what that means and how much money it will require. For example:

> A minimum of $75,000 of income per year in retirement would allow me to make two international trips per year. I will receive $20,000 per year in Social Security and retirement benefits, so I need $55,000 in investment income. Investment earnings from $800,000 would generate the desired income. I want to retire in 10 years.

Having specific goals gives you many advantages. For example, by keeping your eye on the reason for investing, you will focus on the long term and "the big picture," be able to monitor and measure your progress, and be able to determine whether or not your behavior matches your goals.

Strategy 3: Have Quantitative Investment Criteria

Having a set of quantitative investment criteria allows you to avoid investing on emotion, rumor, stories, and other psychologically based biases. It is not the intent of this textbook to recommend a specific investment strategy such as "value" investing or "growth" investing.

Just as it is important to have specific investing goals, it is important to write down specific investment criteria. Before buying a stock, compare the characteristics of the company to your criteria. If a particular stock doesn't meet your criteria, don't invest in it.

Consider the Klondike Investment Club of Buffalo, Wyoming, discussed in Chapter 8. Their number 1 ranking stems in part from the fact that they only make buying decisions based on an acceptable research report. Their criteria keep them from falling prey to their psychological biases. On the other hand, the California Investors Club's lack of success is partially due to their lack of criteria. Their decision process leads to buying decisions that are ultimately controlled by emotion.

Even though quantitative criteria are used, qualitative information also can be important. Information about the quality of the firm's management or the types of new products under development can be useful. If a stock meets your quantitative criteria, then you can examine these qualitative factors.

Strategy 4: Diversify

It is not likely that you will diversify in a manner suggested by modern portfolio theory and discussed in Chapter 6. However, if you keep some simple diversification rules in mind, you can do well.

- *Diversify by owning many different types of stocks.* You can be reasonably well diversified with 15 stocks that are from different industries and are of different size companies. One diversified mutual fund would accomplish this goal, too. However, a portfolio of 50 technology stocks is not a diversified portfolio; neither is one that includes 5 technology mutual funds.
- *Own very little of the firm you work for.* You already have your human capital invested in the firm; that is, your income is dependent on the company. Therefore, diversify your "whole self" by avoiding the company in your investments.
- *Invest in bonds, too.* A diversified portfolio should include some bonds or bond mutual funds.

Diversifying in this way helps investors avoid tragic losses that can truly affect their life. In addition, diversification is a shield against the psychological biases of attachment and familiarity.

Strategy 5: Control Your Investing Environment

If you are on a diet, you should not leave a dish of M&M candies on the table. Similarly, if you want to overcome your psychological investment biases, you should control your investment environment.

So many people are frequently checking their stocks at work that companies are limiting Internet access to employees so they are not distracted. To control your environment, you need to limit the activities that magnify your psychological biases. Here are some ways to help you control your environment.

- *Check your stocks once per month.* By checking your stocks once per month instead of once per hour, the behavioral reactions of snake bite, seeking pride, and playing with the house's money will be inhibited.
- *Make trades only once per month and on the same day of the month.* Pick one day of the month, such as the 15th, and only place buy-and-sell trades on that day. This will help you avoid the misconception that speed is important. Speed is only important if you want to chase a stock on a rumor and get into it just before its bubble bursts. On the other hand, trading once per month helps overcome overconfidence trading.
- *Review your portfolio annually to see how it lines up with your specific goals.* When you review your portfolio, keep in mind the psychological biases of status quo, endowment, representativeness, and familiarity. Does each security in your portfolio contribute to meeting your investment goals and maintaining diversification? Keep records so you can overcome cognitive dissonance and other memory biases.

ADDITIONAL RULES OF THUMB

Consider implementing these rules to shield you from your own psychological biases.

1. Avoid stocks that are selling for less than $5 per share. Most investment scams are conducted in these penny stocks.
2. Chatrooms and message boards are for entertainment purposes only. It is on these boards that your overconfidence is fostered, familiarity is magnified, and artificial "social consensus" is formed.
3. Before you place a trade on a stock that does not meet your criteria, remember that it is unlikely that you know more than the market. Investing outside of your criteria implies that you

have some informational advantage over others. Are you sure you know more?

4. Strive to earn the market return. Most active trading is motivated by the desire to earn a higher return than everyone else is. The strategies for earning a higher return usually foster psychological biases and ultimately contribute to lower returns. However, the strategies for earning the market return, like fully diversifying, are successful because they inhibit your biases.
5. Review the psychological biases annually. This action will reenforce the first strategy of the chapter.

Successful investing is more than just knowing all about stocks. Indeed, understanding yourself is equally important. "Knowledgeable" investors frequently fail because they allow their psychological biases to control their decisions. This chapter illustrates the self-control problem and proposes some strategies for overcoming the psychological biases.

USING BIASES FOR GOOD

Most discussions of psychological biases, including those in this book, focus on how the biases are problems for investors and how they can be overcome. However, by reorganizing the investment process, some biases can be used to help investors. For example, instead of setting up a 401(k) plan process where social and psychological influences inhibit employees from contributing, it might be better to set up the process in ways such that the influences encourage employees to contribute.

The status quo bias causes employees to procrastinate in making their retirement plan decisions. Indeed, many procrastinate so long that they never participate in the plan. Instead of requiring the new employee to take action to enroll, enroll the employee automatically and require the person to take action to disenroll.[13] Instead of exerting an effort to start the participation, employees participate automatically. Those not wishing to participate must make the effort to disenroll. An automatic enrollment policy in a 401(k) savings plan results in substantially more employees participating in the pension plan, although most just stay at the default level of contribution and asset allocation. One problem with this approach is that some of the employees would have participated without the automatic enrollment. In addition, they would have contributed a higher amount and chosen a more aggressive asset allocation than the default money market fund, but they do not change the default allocation because of the status quo bias. Therefore, this automatic enrollment of employees helps many but might harm some.

Richard Thaler and Shlomo Benartzi proposed a four-step approach that they call Save More Tomorrow (SMT) and that overcomes several psychological biases.[14] They suggested that employees who are not contributing to their 401(k) plan can begin to do so by agreeing to the following plan. First, the employee is asked to agree to the plan well in advance; that is, the decision does not have any immediate ramifications. Second, the plan starts by having the employee agree to begin contributing at his or her next pay raise with a small contribution rate, such as 2 percent. By combining a pay raise with the contribution, the employee still sees a small increase in pay but also begins contributing. Third, the employee agrees to increase the contribution rate at each pay raise until a preset maximum level is reached. Fourth, the employee can opt out of the plan at any time. Although the hope is that employees will not opt out, the ability to do so makes them more comfortable about joining the plan. The SMT plan requires the employees to make decisions far in advance, and then the status quo bias works to their advantage because they do not take the option of opting out of the plan.

This plan was tested at a mid-size manufacturing company whose savings participation rate was low. The 315 employees had an average savings rate of 4.4 percent of their earnings. They were asked to increase their contribution by 5 percent. Those employees who claimed they could not contribute the 5 percent were offered the SMT program. The program was made available to 207 employees, and 162 employees agreed to join. These employees had a low savings rate of 3.5 percent, on average. The 153 employees who did not join the SMT plan either did nothing or made a one-time increase in their savings rate. On average, the people who did not adopt the SMT plan had a savings rate of 5.3 percent. The effect of joining the plan was dramatic. After three pay raises, those who had joined the SMT plan had increased their savings rate from 3.5 percent to 11.6 percent. Those who did not join the SMT plan increased their savings rate from 5.3 percent to only 7.5 percent. The dramatic increase in the savings rate associated with the SMT plan was beneficial to those employees because they began saving more for their retirement. It was also beneficial to the managers of the firm because the company was being constrained by the U.S. Department of Labor antidiscrimination rules. Those rules restrict the proportion of retirement contribution that can be made by the higher-income employees when the lower-paid employees have low contribution rates.

The challenge for people in the financial industry is to develop more programs in which people's own psychological biases help them make good decisions instead of bad ones.

Questions

1. How can rules of thumb be used to avoid making psychological bias–induced errors? Give examples.
2. What biases might be overcome by having quantitative criteria?
3. What biases might be overcome by reviewing one's stocks and portfolio infrequently?

End Notes

1. Kenneth Fisher and Meir Statman, "A Behavioral Framework for Time Diversification," *Financial Analysts Journal* (May/June 1999): 92.
2. This discussion is from Richard Thaler and Hersh Shefrin, "An Economic Theory of Self-Control," *Journal of Political Economy* 89(1981): 392–406.
3. This example is proposed in Ted O'Donoghue and Matthew Rabin, "Doing It Now or Later," *American Economic Review* 89(1999): 103–124.
4. George Ainsle, "Derivation of 'Rational' Economic Behavior from Hypoerbolic Discount Curves," *American Economic Review* 81(1991): 334–340.
5. These ideas are explored in Richard Thaler and Hersh Shefrin, "An Economic Theory of Self-Control," *Journal of Political Economy* 89(1981): 392–406; and Stephen Hoch and George Loewenstein, "Time-Inconsistent Preferences and Consumer Self-Control," *Journal of Consumer Research* 17(1991): 492–507.
6. George Akerlof, "Procrastination and Obedience," *American Economic Review* 81(1991): 1–19.
7. Richard Thaler, "Psychology and Savings Policies," *American Economic Review* 84(1994): 186–192.
8. Richard Thaler and Hersh Shefrin, "An Economic Theory of Self-Control," *Journal of Political Economy* 89(1981): 392–406.
9. Benjamin Ayers, Steven Kachelmeister, and John Robinson, "Why Do People Give Interest-Free Loans to the Government? An Experimental Study of Interim Tax Payments," *Journal of the American Taxation Association* 21(1999): 55–74.
10. Richard Thaler, "Psychology and Savings Policies," *American Economic Review* 84(1994): 186–192.
11. Hersh Shefrin and Richard Thaler, "Mental Accounting, Saving, and Self-Control," in *Choice over Time*, edited by George Loewenstein and Jon Elster, New York: Russell Sage Foundation, 1992.
12. This discussion is adapted from Ted O'Donoghue and Matthew Rabin, "Choice and Procrastination," *Quarterly Journal of Economics* 116(2001): 121–160.
13. Brigitte Madrian and Dennis Shea, "The Power of Suggestion: Inertia in 401(k) Participation and Savings Behavior," *Quarterly Journal of Economics* 116(2001): 1149–1187.
14. Richard Thaler and Shlomo Benartzi, "Save More Tomorrow: Using Behavioral Economics to Increase Employee Savings," *Journal of Political Economy*, forthcoming.

Index

Q

R